FROM THE ~~AUTHOR OF~~ CAREERGASM!

CAREER

ROOKIE

A GET-IT-TOGETHER GUIDE
FOR GRADS, STUDENTS,
AND CAREER NEWBIES

SARAH VERMUNT

More Praise for *Career Rookie*

"I love this freakin' book! Sarah Vermunt has written the definitive guide to career success for anyone who wants more from work. Buy a copy for every college student and grad you know."

— Kevin Kruse, *New York Times*–bestselling author of *Great Leaders Have No Rules*

"It's so rare to find a writer who so brilliantly walks the line between no-nonsense real talk and compassionate warmth: Sarah's kindness and enthusiasm shine through with every chapter. I wish *Career Rookie* had existed when I was starting out, because she would've spared me a lot of power cries."

— Anne T. Donahue, bestselling author of *Nobody Cares*

"A must-read for new grads who want to get their career kick-started in the right way!"

— Shannon Lee Simmons, bestselling author of *Worry-Free Money*

"Sarah Vermunt might just be the singular adult on planet Earth who will not lie to you. And take it from a geriatric millennial like myself — weeding out the lying-liars is job numero uno. Best of luck, grasshoppers, may the force of honest AF straight-talkers be with you."

— Steph Jagger, founder of The Great Big Journey and author of *Unbound: Finding Myself on Top of the World*

"Sarah Vermunt has done it again. With joyful irreverence, she kicks garden variety career advice to the curb and shows us the better way: the way to what we truly want."

— Christina Crook, author of *The Joy of Missing Out: Finding Balance in a Wired World*

"This brilliant and salty little volume is so hilarious you'll forget it's actually helping you figure your shit out and go pro."

— Sarah Seidelmann, author of *Born to FREAK: A Salty Primer for Irrepressible Humans*

Praise for *Careergasm*

"What makes Sarah Vermunt's new work manual *Careergasm: Find Your Way to Feel-Good Work* stand out from all the rest is she strips out all the yawn-inducing, sometimes straight-up nonsensical corporate jargon that makes so many other how-to's insufferable, injects just enough casual language to make youngs feel comfortable, and breaks it down into totally digestible, doable, realistic chunks (no abstract "If you dream it, you can achieve it!" mantras here)."

— *FLARE*

"Her advice is spot-on . . . This is an irreverent but important addition to the career shelves."

— *Booklist*

"*Careergasm* is refreshingly real, fiercely empowering, and full of piss and vinegar . . . like the author herself! For a feel-good career that thrills and delights, think of this as FUN required reading!"

— Linda Sivertsen, bestselling author and host of the *Beautiful Writers Podcast*

"*Careergasm* is a fun, energizing, useful tool for the person who wants more from their work than a way to pay bills. Prepare to engage deeply and transform your work!"

— Pamela Slim, author of *Escape from Cubicle Nation* and *Body of Work*

"Passionate, honest, and funny, Sarah Vermunt will take you from having no freaking idea what to do to being super jazzed and running down the path towards work that feels good. There might even be rainbows. There are so many YES! moments, so many gems, so many nuggets of smarts and wisdom in this book. Each one is a little nudge; add them all up and you'll find yourself down the path of a fun and fulfilling career and, just maybe, actually liking Mondays."

— Marc Johns, artist

CAREER ROOKIE

 A GET-IT-TOGETHER GUIDE
FOR GRADS, STUDENTS,
AND CAREER NEWBIES

SARAH VERMUNT

Published by ECW Press
665 Gerrard Street East
Toronto, Ontario, Canada, M4M 1Y2
416-694-3348 / info@ecwpress.com

Purchase the print edition and
receive the eBook free! For details,
go to ecwpress.com/eBook.

Editor for the press: Jen Knoch
Cover design: David A. Gee
Text design: Troy Cunningham
Author photo: Anushila Shaw

LIBRARY AND ARCHIVES CANADA
CATALOGUING IN PUBLICATION

Vermunt, Sarah, 1980-, author
Career rookie : a get-it-together guide for grads,
students and career newbies / Sarah Vermunt.

Issued in print and electronic formats.
ISBN 978-1-77041-488-4 (softcover)
ISBN 978-1-77305-351-6 (PDF)
ISBN 978-1-77305-350-9 (ePub)

1. College graduates—Employment. 2. Young
adults—Employment. 3. School-to-work transition. 4.
Vocational guidance. 5. Job hunting.
I. Title.

HD6277.V47 2019   650.14
C2018-905327-5   C2018-905328-3

The publication of *Career Rookie* has been generously supported by the Government of Ontario through the
Ontario Book Publishing Tax Credit, and through Ontario Creates for the marketing of this book.

PRINTED AND BOUND IN CANADA

PRINTING: MARQUIS   5   4   3   2   1

FOR BRIAN, BRAD, DAN, AND SCOTTIE.
BIG SISTER WAS THE FIRST JOB TITLE I EVER HAD.
STILL ONE OF MY FAVS.

INTRODUCTION
WHAT THE ACTUAL FUCK · 9

INTRODUCTION
WHAT THE ACTUAL FUCK

Hey there. Welcome to the beginning of your career! Maybe you're still hungover from graduation. Or maybe graduation was a few years ago, but you're still feeling dazed and confused. Either way, I know what you're thinking . . .

What the actual fuck. Why didn't anyone tell me it would be like this?

AND

Jesus Christ, is this really all there is?! I busted my ass in school for the last two decades expecting some kind of payoff. #notworthit

AND MAYBE EVEN

What are the rules here? Do I really need to make a LinkedIn profile? Will I have to start washing my hair more often? Do I need to buy a FUCKING PANTSUIT?! Because that is literally my worst nightmare.

You've heard a lot of shitty things about adulthood. Some of it is true — there are bills to pay and pants to wear — but, luckily, some of it is most definitely *not* true.

The first step in getting your career game together is sorting the truth from the life-sucking lies. Those things are tougher to tell apart than you'd think, especially when you're new to your career. Take this doozie, for example:

Everyone else has their shit together.

Nope. Bullshit.
Total bullshit.

And yet you probably feel like this is very true — that you're a gazillion years behind already because everyone else was given some secret playbook for adulting while you weren't looking.

Not so.

Here's the truth: Most people don't know what the hell they're doing straight out of school. And most people feel sick about it because they don't even know what they want, let alone how to get it.

> Here's the truth:
> Most people don't know what the hell they're doing straight out of school. And most people feel sick about it because they don't even know what they want, let alone how to get it.

I know this because I'm a career coach. Every day I work with people who feel paralyzed on the doorstep of their career. People who feel lost, freaked out, and a little bit stabby — confused about which path to take and panicked that they're falling behind. Together we figure out how to dial down the anxiety, decide what they want, and make a solid plan to go after it. That's what you and I will do in the following pages, too. We'll walk through that WTF feeling of starting your career, so you can get clear on what you want and cook up a killer plan to go get it.

Ready? Let's do this.

1
I DON'T KNOW
WHAT I WANT

When you graduate from school and start your career, you're kind of like an animal that's wandered out of the forest onto a busy highway. You see your future rushing toward you, but you feel paralyzed — frozen in the headlights. You know you have to pick a direction and get your ass moving, but you can't feel your legs, so you just stand there, stupefied, thinking, *FUCK FUCK FUCKITY FUCK HOLY FUCK I CAN'T BELIEVE THIS IS HAPPENING TO ME. WHAT THE HELL AM I SUPPOSED TO DO NOW?!*

You're supposed to know which direction to move in, right?

The answer is no. You're not supposed to know which direction to move in. You're not supposed to know what you want or how to get there.

Most of the career rookies I work with feel like epic failures because they don't know what they want. They say things like:

*Why can't I just get my shit together
and pick something already?*

What kind of loser doesn't even know what they like?

*WTF is wrong with me? Shouldn't I
have this figured out by now?*

Not only do they feel lost, but they feel stupid for not having it figured out — ashamed of their uncertainty.

Maybe this is how you feel, too.

But you shouldn't feel ashamed of your uncertainty.

Don't get me wrong, it totally *makes sense* that you would feel ashamed of your uncertainty. For the past 20-odd years, you've had a team of people cheering you on, saying, *Work hard and you can be anything!* We live in a hyped-up, fulfillment-obsessed society that constantly screams *FOLLOW YOUR DREAMS!!!*

But how can you follow your dreams if you don't know what they are?

That's where the shame comes in. You think, *Jesus, after all of this support and encouragement, how do I still not know what I want?* So you assume the problem is you, and the self-flagellation begins.

Here's why the problem isn't you: At the same time as society has been cheerleading you to *follow your dreams*, it has also sternly been pointing its bony finger at you, saying, *Follow the rules*. Those two messages together amount to a weird kind of doublethink that essentially says, *Follow your dreams! As long as they fit into this rigid set of broadly accepted rules!* It's a mindfuck.

When kids are very young, they're encouraged to dream. *I want to be a ballerina when I grow up! I'm going to be a baseball player! I want to make cakes! I want to be president! I'm going to be a singer!*

Aw, isn't that sweet, people think, saying, *Good for you! Dream big, kiddo!*

How can you follow your dreams if you don't know what they are?

But at some point, the societal doublethink kicks in, and words like *rules* and *should* and *practical* become more important. Suddenly we're forced to choose between *should* and *want*. And since the loving adults in our lives want us to be safe, they gently guide us to fall in line. This happens earlier than you might think.

The other day I was waiting to pick up a friend at the bus station. A little boy and his mother were siting in the bank of chairs behind me. As he played with his crayons, he said to his mom, "I'm going to be an artist when I grow up!"

"No, honey. That's not a real job," his mom said.

"Oh," said the kid.

"You can work at a bank like Daddy! Or you can be an architect! Wouldn't that be fun?"

"What's an architect?"

"Architects get to draw pictures of big buildings."

"Oh, okay," said the kid, and he went on with his coloring. He didn't seem discouraged or upset or even like he had been paying much attention to the conversation, but the seed was planted. He was six.

Fifteen years from now, that kid could be graduating from art school or design school, but instead he'll probably be graduating from business school or engineering school with a weird feeling in the pit of his stomach, thinking, *Something doesn't feel right. I'm not really sure if I want this. On the other hand, I don't know what I DO want.*

And that feeling will be 100% legit. He doesn't know what he wants because he wasn't allowed to want it. Years of even the most gentle and loving conditioning will do that to you. In fact, most of us at one time or another have been told that we're not allowed to want what we want — whether it was by a parent or teacher or society at large, and whether it was said sternly or gently.

That's how you lose touch with your desire. You push it down because it's not allowed. You start following the rules and doing everything "right." You adjust your expectations and dream *appropriately*. And then you slog it out in school

16

for at least 15 years, and then graduate and wonder, *How do I not know what I want? What is WRONG with me?*

It's not you, honey. It's them.

➽ CAUTIONARY TALES ➽

So you don't know what you want. (We'll get there, I promise.) But you know what you *don't* want: a job that makes you want to walk off the edge of a tall building. You don't want to settle, but you don't want to chase some impossible pipe dream either. You don't want to go to some shit job every day that makes you feel bored or frustrated or burned out or like you're selling a little piece of your soul with each passing Monday. You know those people. It's your mom/dad/Uncle Jim/every other sorry schmuck who hates their job.

Figuring out what you want for your career is a lot of pressure off the bat, especially when you're feeling clueless. But you know what's easier? Getting clear on what you *don't* want. That's a good place to start because some of that stuff is probably on your radar already. I can almost guarantee that there are some people in your life that you look at and think, *Yikes, that is SO not for me. Not in a million years. Gawd no.* Their career seems dull or too stressful or like a full-blown dumpster fire, and, frankly, you don't wanna go out like that.

Maybe you're thinking you don't want a career like your dad's. Because the dude works all the time, and you hardly remember what he looks like. Or maybe it's your best friend. He always said he wanted to do something creative, and he ended up working in payroll. WTF?! Or maybe it's your older sister. She never took the time to figure out what she wanted and just did what your mom told her to do. Technically, she's doing everything "right," but you get the sense that she's not happy.

A client I'll call Maya — none of the names I'm using here are real, but the stories are — was encouraged to apply for a master's degree by one of her professors. And to help pay for it, she could even work in his lab. A master's degree and a guaranteed job to help pay it off didn't sound too shabby. But Maya noticed that her professor was fairly isolated in that lab. Maya was a social butterfly and wasn't especially psyched about the solitary nature of lab work or, for that matter, the area of study. So even though she didn't know what she *did* want, that particular option was a no for Maya.

Another client, Jerome, was groomed for the family business. In fact, he already knew his father's business inside out because he'd grown up in it. He now had a business degree and would be even *more* prepared to take over the business. But he had major reservations. He had no interest in living the lifestyle that his father had. He couldn't remember a single family holiday that wasn't interrupted by his father having to tend to some urgent business need, and he'd be damned if that was going to be his life, too. So instead of falling in line and doing what was expected of him, he said no.

Sometimes having a clear picture of what you *don't* want

keeps you from accidentally straying down the wrong path. The people you think of and think, *Yuck, I SO do not want that life* may be lovely people, but for now let them serve as cautionary career tales.

🖎 UNDER PRESSURE 🖎

Your Aunt Marg spots you at the family barbeque. You know exactly what's coming, so you try to make a run for it, but she's too quick, and she pins you between the lemonade and the dessert table. You haven't seen her since graduation, and she wastes no time getting straight to the point. Less than 30 seconds into the awkward conversation, she utters the four words most dreaded by twentysomethings everywhere: *So what's your plan?*

You mutter, "Oh, you know, I'm just exploring some options." But what you really want to do is karate chop her in the neck and drown her in her own bean dip while screaming, *I DON'T HAVE A PLAN! I CAN'T EVEN THINK FAR ENOUGH AHEAD TO MAKE A GODDAMN GROCERY LIST! STOP PRESSURING ME ALREADY!!!* *runs screaming through a brick wall, Wile E. Coyote style, never to be seen again*

So what's your plan?

What's next?

How's the job hunt going?

Got anything lined up yet?

Questions like this probably make you want to go on a weeklong bender. *SO. MUCH. PRESSURE.* Why the hell does everyone have to get all up in your grill like that?! When you're feeling lost and stuck about your career, suddenly it seems like the whole damn world is keeping tabs on you. People like:

CLUELESS SMALL TALKERS. These people aren't intentionally trying to stress you out. In fact, they probably aren't even aware that you're stressed. It's just that they don't know what else to say to you. It's people like your Aunt Marg or Uncle Jerry, who you only see once a year during the holidays. When people don't know you that well or don't know what to talk about, they'll often reach for the ol' *how's work going?* question, which, while fairly boring, is usually harmless. They're not trying to fuck with you or apply pressure, so just let it slide, give a short vague answer, and change the subject.

BUTTON PUSHERS. Now, these people *are* trying to fuck with you. And it's because they're insecure. I'm talking about your friend Melissa, who spends two hours over brunch every weekend sharing gossip and digging for more. Or your former classmate Jackie, who texts occasionally but always with an opening line like, *OMG you won't belieeeeeve what I* *just heard about so-and-so.* I'd put good money on Melissa and Jackie being button pushers — people who love drama and get off on the struggle and misfortune of others so they can feel better about themselves. Pay attention, and the next time you're at brunch, you'll swear you notice a smile curling at Melissa's lips as she asks, *Sooooo, how's the job hunt going?* Hopefully, you aren't friends with many people like this. If you are, you have *got* to find a better brunch crew. Or even better, say you have to go to the bathroom mid-meal and stiff her on the bill.

LOVING ALLIES. These people live at the other end of the spectrum. They actually and genuinely give a shit. These are probably people like your mom and dad and boyfriend or girlfriend and most of your close friends. Maybe they can see that you're struggling, and they just want to check in and see if you're okay. And they want to help if they can. GOD. BLESS. THESE. PEOPLE. Try not to get too triggered when they ask how you're doing and how the job search is going. They care, and they're on your side.

LOVING ALLIES DISGUISED AS ASSHOLES. Maybe your mom calls you about your job search every day. Or maybe your sister passive-aggressively emails you 30 job posts for things you clearly have no interest in even though you've asked her to stop. Or maybe every time you see your dad, you're subjected to a preachy speech about "taking responsibility for yourself," and by the way, did you hear that so-and-so's son

Neil just got into med school, and why can't you be more like Neil? My guess is that your loved ones and family members and especially your parents just want you to be okay. They love you. But they (mistakenly) believe that the best way to make you okay is to apply more pressure. (After all, it works for diamonds?) Try to remember that these people are probably loving allies behaving badly because they don't know any better. Tell them how you feel. Or at least stop taking all of those calls.

It's not like you're not putting enough pressure on yourself already. You'd happily get your shit together career-wise if only you knew what you wanted. But instead of having a vision and a plan for your career, you've got food court daze . . .

◢◤ FOOD COURT DAZE ◥◣

Food court daze is that unfocused, slack-jawed daze you fall into in food courts. Should you get a burrito or a burger? Sushi? A sandwich? Pizza? There are too many options, and suddenly you're incapable of making good life choices. You find yourself in line at Taco Bell and wonder where it all went wrong.

Starting your career can feel like that, too. There are just too many options and things can get blurry and over-whelming very quickly. If you're feeling a bit of food court daze when it comes to your career, it helps to talk out your options with someone. Or even just write 'em down — all the stuff you're even mildly considering, even if you're not sure which option (if any) you should go for. Sales gig? Marketing internship? Learn a trade? Work for a start-up? Screw it and go back to school? Who the hell knows?

The point isn't to know with striking clarity right away. The point is to get the jumbled mess of ideas out of your head and onto paper, or into the ear of someone you trust. (Ideally, someone who will just listen, not tell you what to do.)

The point isn't to know with striking clarity right away.

You don't have to choose *any* of the options currently on your mind if you don't want to. BTW, we're not even *close* to having to pick something yet. We just started, bro. We're just trying to bring some order to things, so you feel a little less dazed.

Now, sometimes the problem isn't just feeling overwhelmed about which option to pick; sometimes the problem is anxiety about picking anything at all — fear of picking option X instead of Y or Z, which boils down to:

But what if I pick X and regret it because I really should have picked Y?!

23

Choosing one door means closing others, and that's stressful. Because if you get a burrito, you can't also get a burger or sushi or a sandwich or pizza. Picking something means excluding other things, and maybe you'd rather keep your options open.

Here's the trouble with that line of thinking: You're going to get hungry eventually. Which means that you *will* have to pick something eventually. Better to thoughtfully consider your options now instead of hungrily grasping after something in a panicked last-minute fit of desperation.

But before we really start exploring your options, let's get honest about *why* you're feeling lost and what exactly it is you're struggling with . . .

➡ THE STRUGGLE IS REAL ⬅

There are a handful of reasons why people feel stuck at the beginning of their careers. These are the biggies:

● I HAVE NO IDEA WHAT I EVEN LIKE.

This was my own experience after graduation. I studied journalism, but over the course of my studies I discovered I did not want to be a journalist. So there I was: lost AF, with no idea what I liked, only the knowledge of what I *didn't* like. Maybe that's where you are right now, too.

Choosing one door
means closing others,
and that's stressful.

● I WANT TOO MANY DIFFERENT THINGS.

This might be you if you want to be an interior designer *and* a web designer *and* a massage therapist *and* a yoga instructor, and you just can't bear the thought of not doing *all* of the things. (This goes back to the fear of closing doors.) Or maybe you have "shiny object syndrome." You feel insanely passionate about one career idea for exactly one hot second before you're swept away, enraptured with something even more desirable. Your passion is hot but flaky and wildly inconsistent.

● I KNOW WHAT I WANT, BUT IT DOESN'T EXACTLY PAY THE BILLS (AT LEAST NOT RIGHT AWAY).

Maybe you want to write a book. Or make an app. Or design your own line of stationery. Or write and produce your own musical. That stuff will take a LONG-ASS WHILE before it starts making you any money. And in the meantime, you gotta find a way to pay for your Lucky Charms.

● I KNOW WHAT I WANT, JUST NOT HOW TO GET IT.

This is probably you if you went to school for accounting but actually want to be a screenwriter. Or if you want to open your own flower shop. Or start a furniture business using reclaimed wood. Some career paths are fairly prescribed, and the steps to get there are formalized and obvious (like for accountants and lawyers and engineers), and some aren't (like for screenwriters and florists and furniture designers).

• I KIND OF KNOW WHAT I WANT, BUT I'M SCARED SHITLESS TO ADMIT IT.

This might be you if what you want is wildly different than the path you're on right now. Or if what you want is a huge long shot. Or if it's something your family or friends might disapprove of. It's less about being lost and more about being in denial. Letting yourself want what you want and considering the possibility of actually going after it scares the pants off you. And you're not sure what's worse — the possibility of failure or being chickenshit and never going after what you want.

No matter which category feels like you, we're going to cover that in the rest of this book.

Not sure what you like? We're going to do a deep dive and get you back in touch with your desire.

Want a lot of different things or something that doesn't pay the bills (yet)? We're going to talk about parallel tracks, so you can do what you want *and* pay the rent.

Know what you want but not how to get it? We're going to do some research and make a plan, Stan.

Know what you want, but you're scared shitless to admit it? We're going to address your fear. Because not *admitting* what you want isn't the same thing as not *knowing* what you want. Denial and uncertainty are two different things.

So you know what your main struggle is right now, but we're still a long way off from knowing what you want and having a plan to go after it. Which is totally fine because one thing at a time. This'll take a while.

Denial and uncertainty are two different things.

Maybe what you should do next is sit back and wait for a sign, right?

Nope.

Waiting for a sign is not an effective strategy. Oh, don't get me wrong, signs are great, and they're totally out there, but if they haven't pointed you in the right direction yet, you can't just keep waiting. (Because you'll have to pay off that student debt sometime, and you need a J.O.B.)

So instead of waiting for the signs to show up in all of their neon flashing glory, we're going to actively hunt those fuckers down.

Pack your sense of adventure. We move at dawn.

2
SWIPE RIGHT

areer signs — signs from the universe about what you should do with your career — don't come in the form of specific job titles lit up in neon lights. They don't club you over the head and drag you to your dream job. Career signs are a little subtler than that.

Most career signs show up as inklings and whispers and curiosities. And it goes without saying that you need to pay attention and actually notice the signs for them to be of any good to you. If noticing signs isn't your forte, no problem. We're going to keep it simple and just sort some career ingredients into two simple piles — yes please, and no thanks.

If only scoring your ideal career was as simple as hitting up Tinder. It's not, but I'd like you to play along with me anyway. We're going to look at the stuff you find attractive in a career (swipe right) and also some of the stuff you find unattractive (swipe left), and we're going to consider three different categories — work activities, work peeps, and work vibe.

➽ YOUR WORK ACTIVITIES ⬅

Let's start with the easiest and most obvious stuff — the workish activities you do and don't like to do. You get to decide when to swipe right (yes please!) and swipe left (no thanks). Now, since you haven't worked much yet, you may have to go on a hunch. But the good news is your hunches are almost *always* right. So don't second-guess yourself. Trust your hunches.

Need some help to get started? Here are some of my own preferences for work activities: I don't like boring, repetitive tasks, so nothing makes me want to swipe left like most administrative work. That stuff nearly throws me into a fit like a toddler who's been told he can't bring his lightsaber to church. Same goes for most kinds of reporting and research. Also, most statistical work and any super complicated technical work frustrates the hell out of me. We're talking assembling Ikea furniture–level frustrated. Grocery store self-checkout frustrated. No thanks. Swipe left.

On the other hand, there are some work activities I always find myself attracted to: teaching and nurturing, helping people grow, writing, telling stories, noticing patterns,

Trust your hunches.

connecting seemingly unrelated ideas, and creating systems to organize complicated things. All of that stuff is a hell yes for me. Swipe right.

What are some work activities that feel like a hell yes to you? And what are some that really turn you off? It's okay if some of the things you think of seem vague.

Don't be surprised if some of the stuff on my swipe-right list is on your swipe-left list or vice versa, or if you think of work activities I haven't touched upon (because the options are pretty much endless). There are gazillions of things people do at work, and everybody likes something different. You do you.

For example, Kelsey is obsessed with numbers, specifically financial data. The woman's face lights up like a goddamn Christmas tree when she talks about it. I asked her what it is she loves so much about it, and she said, "Numbers tell a story. Not individual numbers themselves, but when various bits of financial data come together they tell a story." Kelsey is meticulous and loves digging into things and finding mistakes. She loves playing detective where numbers are involved — poking around and piecing things together until a story emerges. She's a real estate underwriter and LOVES it.

Michelle is another client of mine, and one particular thing was at the top of her work activity list — movement. She knew that she would slowly die inside if she had to spend eight hours a day behind a desk. So every single career she considered — landscaper, fitness instructor, arborist, personal trainer, and many others — involved physical movement.

Maybe you're pretty sure you'd like some of the work activities related to the field you studied (which is ideal), but you're not sure which work activities you'd like *the most*. Omar is a business grad who is curious about how people think and behave. He sees people as puzzles. With his interest in how people think, his charisma, and his ability to easily understand what people need, everybody told Omar he'd be amazing at sales. He sensed he would be good at sales, too, and his dad even had a hookup for a job. But while the idea of sales was intriguing to Omar, he was even more interested in marketing. He sensed that both sales and marketing would be good fits for him. It felt kind of like choosing between a brownie and a chocolate chip cookie — both good options, but you still gotta pick one. Because marketing was *more* desirable than sales to him, that's the direction he chose.

Everybody likes something different. You do you.

Once you have a sense of what general work activities you'd enjoy, you'll want to get even more specific. Like Omar, Jane was interested in marketing. She completed a Bachelor of Commerce in Marketing at school but wasn't quite sure what to do with it when she graduated. Should she work in digital marketing, event-based marketing, experiential marketing, or marketing research? And should she work at an agency or as a part of an in-house marketing team for a company? It was like deciding on a chocolate chip cookie but getting really specific about what *kind*. Double chocolate? Sea salted milk chocolate? Oatmeal chocolate chip? After gathering more information (using a technique you'll learn about in chapter three), Jane made her choice and went with experiential marketing because she sensed she'd like it the most.

The whole point of getting clear on which work tasks you think you would and wouldn't like is to increase your odds of choosing a job you'll actually enjoy. You don't want to land in a gig that makes you feel like you're gonna fall asleep under your desk by 10 a.m. Or one that makes you feel more jittery than a 4 p.m. cup of coffee. No job is perfect, but if you're going to do something for eight hours a day, you should feel jazzed about most of it.

Work activities tend to be people's primary focus when thinking about career stuff. But when you stop there, you're missing a big part of the picture. There are two other kinds of things that can really make or break a feel-good career: the people you work with — your colleagues, customers, and clients — and your work environment or vibe — that is, the systems and cultures and spaces you work within. We'll start with your work people and get to the vibe piece in a second.

➠ YOUR WORK PEEPS ⬅

The people you choose to surround yourself with at work —
your colleagues, customers, and clients — can really impact
how you feel. You won't always necessarily have control over
the kind of people around you at work, but if you can get
clear on who your kind of people are and who they're not,
you're much more likely to align with people who have good
vibes and won't drive you nuts.

A little bit about my own preferred peeps to get you
started . . .

I don't like being around or working with people who
are pushy or inconsiderate. Rigid rule followers and people
who are too buttoned up drive me crazy. Same for attention
seekers. I find them exhausting. I don't like being around
people who are all jacked up and super competitive . . . mostly
because that triggers my own competitiveness, and I don't
like how that feels. And the worst kind of people for me to be
around are the *poor me* victim mindset crowd. Those people
feel like energy vampires to me. Too much time around them
makes me feel like a wet noodle. All of these types of people
are a swipe left for me. Nope.

I love people who don't take themselves too seriously —
people who like to make work fun, who naturally look on the
bright side, and who laugh a lot. I also love weirdos — those
quirky oddball types who are comfortable enough in their
own skin to rock an unconventional vibe and do their own

damn thing. But none of these attributes matter to me if the people around me are not also real, and open, and warm. Those qualities are at the very top of my swipe-right list.

Over to you. What qualities and attributes do you find really attractive in people? And what kind of people would you rather not be around and work with? I mean, you probably don't want to be working for Cruella de Vil, right? But let's say you need to be around people with lots of personality. In that case, you're not exactly going to be living your best life if your coworkers are basically a bunch of sentient calculators. Or let's say you like a nice, chill, friendly vibe among colleagues. In that case, you don't want to be working for someone who takes a regular Tuesday morning meeting to dial up the drama to an 11.

Getting clear on who your people *aren't* might be the easier place to start. Take Logan, for example. He scored a job right after graduation, and while it's in a field he's interested in, he's realizing that the people he has to work closest with are *not* his people. Logan is an ideas guy. He wants to innovate and think of ways to improve things. But, unfortunately, Logan works with a team of status quo, *if it ain't broke don't fix it* people. They have no interest in discussing Logan's ideas or even sharing their own. As a result, Logan is bored out of his mind. He's working with the wrong people.

Karin could have shared the same fate as Logan, but she dodged a bullet. She's one of those people who is equally right-brained and left-brained — both wildly creative and expressive and also extremely calculating and analytical. Karin scored a job in fashion (a job she knows many would kill for) but one that didn't quite feel right. She wondered if she might feel better working at a more traditional organization in a job that was more analytical. So she interviewed for a prestigious job at a big multinational tech corporation. The interview lasted a whole day, but she realized it was a mistake 20 minutes in when she thought, *These are so NOT my people!* She learned she feels best working with artists and creatives — just not in the fashion industry — so she's now happily pursuing photography.

When considering who your people are, you may want to consider not only the people you work for and with (bosses and colleagues) but also the people you serve (customers and clients). Audrey is a client of mine who feels passionate about helping people who are struggling to navigate workplace politics. Another client, Uma, feels strongly about helping people with health and wellness, specifically emotional wellness.

To like the tasks of your job often isn't enough. The people around you at work every day can make or break how you feel. So think long and hard about your ideal work posse, and you'll increase your odds of aligning with a true ride-or-die crew of feel-good peeps.

> The people around you at work every day can make or break how you feel.

➡ YOUR WORK VIBE ⬅

We should also talk about the vibe of your work, which I know sounds kinda vague and granola, but it's important. Your work vibe has a lot to do with the kind of energy surrounding your work, which is often a product of the systems and cultures and environments you find yourself in.

For example, I love having lots of autonomy, doing work that is mostly self-directed, which I can organize and plan on my own terms. I like to focus deeply on just one thing for a long stretch of time. I also really enjoy intimacy, so I like building work relationships with people (in my case, my clients) where we trust each other and where we can both be ourselves. My physical work environment also really matters to me. I dig open spaces that have a warm, welcoming vibe. All of that stuff is a big swipe right for me.

Traditional corporate environments are not my thing. I don't like rigid rules or high-pressure situations. Hard pass. That stuff makes me feel like an angry monkey in a small cage. I hate being interrupted or feeling rushed, and I don't like juggling too many things at once or switching tasks frequently. I want to kick ass at whatever I do, so unclear expectations drive me crazy. So do large groups. I find them exhausting. Swipe left.

What about you? Which kinds of work environments, systems, and cultures do you find yourself naturally attracted to? And which ones are a turnoff? Again, you may have to go on a hunch, so use your intuition and whatever experience you have.

Work culture is the most important factor for some people. Max and Nadine came to me from very different industries but with the exact same problem — burnout. Both had graduated only a couple of years ago and landed in organizations that drove them into the ground. In Nadine's case, this slave-driving mentality was pervasive throughout the culture of the organization. Her colleagues were dropping like flies, getting sick and injured and struggling with mental health because the pace at which they were expected to work wasn't sustainable. For Max, on the other hand, the problem wasn't organization-wide, but rather overworking was the culture of her specific team. As a result, finding a job working for organizations and teams with a supportive, reasonably paced work culture was at the very top of both of their lists.

Wes studied psychology and was on track to become a counselor, but he sensed it wasn't the right fit. The work would be too isolating, and the one-on-one interactions he'd have with clients wouldn't be the ideal kind for him. Wes had been a varsity athlete in school and missed the camaraderie and kinship of playing a team sport. He wanted to be a part of a tight-knit team in his work, too — ideally at a large company with many opportunities to develop his leadership and move up. Wes is now part of an investment team at a large bank and finally has the team environment he was looking for.

Sometimes the work environments you might feel drawn to can be very specific. Marley is a client of mine who was a teacher but hated the work environment. Even though she was surrounded by 30 children all day, she felt isolated with not enough interaction with adults. Instead, she felt drawn to start-up culture, so she pursued working for a start-up. I've had clients who felt called to work in environments as specific as hospitals, athletic stadiums, and television studios. I even had one client who was obsessed with the airport. (A place most of us can't wait to leave!) She couldn't get enough of that place and explored every possible option that was airport-related.

That last example brings me to an important point regarding where you work . . .

⟫ SOMETIMES *WHERE* TRUMPS *WHAT* ⟪

What I mean by that is some people care so deeply about *where* they work that it actually supersedes *what* they do for work in terms of importance. And I don't mean where in terms of which company; I mean where as in *where in the world* — which city or country or region. Sometimes, where you want to build your life matters more than exactly what you do for your career. Like if surfing is your biggest passion in life, maybe downtown Chicago isn't where you belong. And if skiing is important to you, you might want to live and work near the mountains.

A client of mine — Fatima — is a major hippie. She hates wearing shoes because they feel too restrictive and she feels disconnected from the earth when she wears them. Unfortunately, Fatima lived in one of the largest, most urban cities in the world and was really freaking miserable because of it. Once we discovered that most of her unhappiness stemmed from being in the wrong *place*, it was just a matter of making a plan to get the hell out. She now lives in a small nature-based community on the West Coast (and doesn't have to wear shoes nearly as often).

> Sometimes, where you want to build your life matters more than exactly what you do for your career.

Another client of mine — Sasha — went to school in New York and moved back home to Toronto after she graduated. She missed New York like crazy. She considered several career options and was fairly open to many things, as long as they brought her back to New York. She chose one of those options and is living in New York now.

At the other end of the spectrum is Eden. She's dying to leave the big city and move to a little rural community. She feels disconnected in cities and hates the fast pace of life. Living in a hectic city makes her feel like she's living inside a dystopian fantasy novel. So she's hatching a plan and quietly plotting her escape to greener pastures.

Literally. I have a brother who's just like Eden. He knew an urban lifestyle wasn't for him, and so he built a life in a rural community. He's happier there. It's the opposite for me. A rural community doesn't feel like the right place for me (even though I grew up on a farm), so I choose city life. You should honor what feels good for you.

Some people don't feel compelled to put down roots in any one place but rather to travel around the world while working. This wasn't really an option 20 years ago, but thanks to technology there are more and more mobile jobs. You can video chat with head office in San Francisco from a hotel room in Dubai or a café in Amsterdam. It's not always as glamorous as it seems, and it's not for everyone (as a certified homebody, just the thought of not having a home base is enough to liquefy my bowels), but if traveling the world is at the very top of your list, mobile work might be something to consider.

▨ DELETED SCENES AND THE HIGHLIGHT REEL ◀▨

Now that you're a little clearer on the work activities, people, and vibes you do and don't like, let's take a look at your work history for more clues . . .

Work history! But I'm just starting my career! I don't HAVE a work history!

Not true.

You may not have a super impressive resume yet, or a long list of full-time jobs, but you definitely have a work history. And you may not even know it, but you've learned a thing or two about what you like and don't like based on your past experiences.

So what counts as your work history? For our purposes, pretty much everything. I'm talking about every little thing you've ever done to make some cash, thinking as far back as you can remember — babysitting, cutting grass, waiting tables, working at the local golf course, painting houses, retail jobs, working as a teaching assistant, all of it.

Let's also include volunteer work — the stuff you did to rack up community service hours in high school, unpaid internships, collecting money for charity, and any volunteer work you did for a cause you care about.

And let's also include things you did just for fun. These are things you probably wouldn't put on your resume, but we'll use them for our own purposes — things like clubs and organizations and teams you were/are a part of (e.g., school newspaper, book club, track team, comedy group, theatre performances) and fun things you do on your own (e.g., reading, photography, making a web series, hiking, graphic design, painting, anything at all).

If you're finding it hard to keep all of that stuff in your head — all the jobs, all the volunteer work, all the clubs and sports and activities — write it down. Cuz we're gonna do something juicy with that list.

Maybe you loved the quiet solitude of cutting grass for

hours, or your fun coworkers from the golf course, or motivating your track teammates, or creating the perfect scene for your web series, or how your volunteer coordinator always asked you for your ideas. Try to think of at least one thing you liked about each job, volunteer gig, or activity — the highlights.

Now do the opposite. Think of the stuff you *didn't* like about your jobs, volunteer work, and activities — the shit you'd happily delete from your memory, the stuff that didn't make the cut.

It's important to be specific. Don't just remember that you hated that your boss was an asshat. Get specific. Like maybe it was that your boss didn't trust you, or he micromanaged or was disorganized or rude.

If you think carefully about what you didn't like, you'll probably see some themes emerge. The shit that drives you nuts almost always follows some kind of pattern. Same for the stuff that lights you up.

For example, if I were to think about my own work highlights, I'd notice that I love anything that involves teaching, and also helping people with problems, and writing (which I do when I blog, write a book, write web copy, or develop content for a course). Those are consistent highlights for me. You may notice some of these themes came up in my swipe-right list as well.

If I were to make a list of the things I've hated, I'd see some themes there, too. For example, much of my work history has shown that I hate high-pressure situations. I hate getting all up in someone's grill and hustling for the upsell or pressuring them to close the deal. I also hate research. I find it boring and tedious and isolating . . . a total snoozefest. My years of babysitting as a teen tell me that working with kids isn't really my thing. Watching two 10-year-olds play basketball on the net screwed to the garage makes me want to nap indefinitely.

> The shit that drives you nuts almost always follows some kind of pattern. Same for the stuff that lights you up.

Your turn. Think about the stuff you enjoyed and the stuff that sucked. Some themes will likely pop out at you. These themes are career clues, pointing out what you do and don't like. These kinds of clues are *pure gold* (even though you probably don't know what to do with them yet). These clues will help you navigate your career. So will these next things we're going to talk about . . .

⇒ HIGH FIVES, HUGS, AND FIST BUMPS ⇐

What are the things you're recognized for most frequently? And what are the things people always seem to thank you for? In other words, where do you always seem to get high fives, hugs, and fist bumps?

We're going to look at that stuff. Not to inflate your ego (though it kinda will), but because the things you're most recognized and appreciated for are often very good career clues.

One of my clients — I'll call him Jake — is easily able to tune in to the abilities and potential of other people. He does this quickly and seemingly effortlessly, even with people he doesn't know very well. It's like he has a special sixth sense for noticing people's best qualities and how they could practically apply them. People are always amazed by and grateful for his insights, and they tell him so. It's no surprise then that Jake is a successful recruiter, placing amazing people into just the right jobs.

Chuck is another client of mine. He's always getting thanked for being a wonderful host. He takes care to plan gatherings down to the finest little detail. And once his parties are in full swing, you'll find him roaming around introducing people to each other, refilling drinks, and making everyone feel comfortable. Chuck realized that his interpersonal warmth and his love of details aren't limited to hosting; he's on the hunt for work in training and development, helping new teams get to know each other, get comfortable, and settle in — playing the same role he does as party host but in a career context.

Gail has an incredible knack for bringing uncomfortable issues out into the open. She gets people to move past their discomfort and to openly discuss taboo issues like workplace sexual harassment and institutionalized racism. The people around her appreciate her ability to make them feel safe and open around such difficult subjects. Gail uses this particular superpower in her consulting work helping organizations raise and address difficult issues.

Now it's your turn. What kind of things do people tend to recognize and thank you for? Where do you get a fist bump, a pat on the back, a handshake, a hug, or a high five? Try to think of at least three things. At first, they might seem totally unrelated to work on the surface (like Chuck's flair for hosting), but that's okay.

Jake's ability to notice potential is really due to the fact that he pays close attention and is very perceptive. Chuck has a flair for hosting because he loves the little details, and also because he's relationally focused and wants to make people feel comfortable and get to know each other. Gail's knack for helping people deal with difficult taboo issues is really rooted in the fact that she's nonjudgmental and makes people feel safe.

What kind of things do people tend to recognize and thank you for?

Chances are the things you're recognized and appreciated for (even if they seem totally unrelated to the work world) are rooted in something deeper, too. Like maybe your knack for furniture placement or pulling together the perfect outfit is really rooted in the fact that you notice how different pieces and details can come together — you have an aesthetic eye. Or maybe you're the person all of your friends go to when they need to talk out a problem. Maybe that's rooted in your ability to listen and ask good questions. Or maybe your ability to plan the perfect vacation is rooted in the fact that you're a details person, and you love to forecast and organize.

These special gifts of yours are like little gems that can be of value to you in the work world. When used in the right way, they'll really help you shine.

3
CAREER INSPO

There's a question I almost always ask my clients over the course of our work together: "Who inspires you? Who do you admire? Who do you dig because of their vibe?"

"Like, people whose careers I want?" they'll ask.

"No. I mean *anybody* — alive or dead, people you know or don't know, celebrities, fictional characters, *anybody*. List a few people."

Sometimes they'll come at me with the names of friends of classmates or relatives. Mom is a popular choice. (For heaven's sake, if you admire your mother, please *tell* her.) But often people go the celebrity route. Beyoncé! Oprah! Ellen! RuPaul! (If someone is easily identified by first name only, you can bet your ass they show up on people's lists.)

Next question: "Why? Why do you love these people? What is it about them that inspires you?"

I have literally never received the answer, *Because they're famous and have a crapload of cash*. Not ever. People go way deeper with their answers. Which is exactly the point.

Take Pete, for example. Anthony Bourdain was at the very top of his inspiration list. If you don't know who Anthony Bourdain was, he was basically a celebrity chef bad boy — a foul-mouthed former heroin addict whose hilarious-as-hell, unfiltered, oh-my-god-I-can't-believe-he-just-said-that attitude somehow managed to come off as charming, magnetic even. He was the celebrity chef version of that person you know is bad for you but who you'd definitely sleep with anyway.

There were a zillion other celebrity rebels that Pete could have admired — Rihanna, Kanye, Quentin Tarantino, Sarah Silverman, Eminem — but it was Anthony Bourdain who did it for him. Pete was also obsessed with a certain food critic. And was inspired by a food stylist photographer on Instagram.

Are you connecting the dots?

Pete was obsessed with *food* and the people who get to *work* with food. He had no desire to become a chef (he knew he'd hate working in a kitchen), but he longed to work with food in some creative way — specifically, to tell stories about food through film or photography or writing.

Sometimes the people who inspire you will converge together to form a big, neon flashing arrow that says, *THIS!!! THIS RIGHT HERE! DO THIS!*

But in the interest of keeping it real, I should tell you that's the exception, not the rule. This inspirational figures thing usually takes a little more detective work before you gather enough clues to make sense of it. But like a Tootsie Pop, where you have to work your way through the hard shell before getting to the soft, chewy center, it's always worth it.

Hayley is an interesting example. Hayley has a brilliant mind and wants an unconventional life. She says she feels like a caged animal any time she has to conform. Life had thrown her a couple of curveballs, but she had always handled them. In fact, she was able to deal with virtually any challenge that came at her. Her strength was seemingly limitless.

Two names were at the top of Hayley's inspirational figures list, both of them fictional — Sarah Connor, waitress turned hero warrior against a military cyborg takeover in the movie *The Terminator*, and Ellen Ripley, the cool-headed, ovaries-of-steel, space-army advisor from the movie *Alien*, who basically saves all of humanity after an alien encounter destroys her ship and kills all of her crew. Talk about a couple of badass bitches.

Now, Hayley wasn't likely to come across a job posting for "Gunslinging Intergalactic Rebel Warrior Fighting to Save the Future of the Human Race." So what to do?

Let's not forget the next question: *Why? Why do you love these people? What is it about them that inspires you?*

Hayley admired that Sarah Connor and Ellen Ripley faced insane challenges and took control. She admired that they were living rebellious lifestyles way outside the norm.

And that they were sharp and intellectual and calculating and unconventional. They were the heroes of their own lives (not to mention saving humanity), brave as fuck, and they got. shit. done. Check, check, check. It was all super inspiring.

"What do you think that tells you about yourself?" I asked.

long pause

"Oh my god, that's what I want, too!" she said. "To tackle a big challenge and take control. And to live kind of a rebellious life."

"And what about those qualities you mentioned — sharp, intellectual, calculating, unconventional, brave?"

"That's me. That's exactly me. Holy shit."

That *was* Hayley. She shared those qualities and was dying to put them to use in her work. She needed a WAY BIGGER challenge to tackle — something that was intellectually stimulating, where she could use her brilliant analytical mind. And, importantly, she wanted to work in a way that didn't force her to conform to anyone else's goddamn rules, to work in a way where she could flex her rebellious side, answering to nobody but herself. She's now a badass entrepreneur, biting off challenge after challenge every day, killing it in her business, and never having to answer to the man.

The most interesting list of inspirational figures I have ever heard, by far, came from Wen — a mild-mannered, kind, clever, strategically minded client of mine. Her list:

- Maleficent, antagonist and self-proclaimed Mistress of All Evil who cursed Sleeping Beauty.
- Penny, the resourceful and precocious junior detective from the children's show *Inspector Gadget*, who uses her fancy video watch and computer book (back in the day before those became *actual* things) to solve every case, despite the bumbling antics of her Uncle Gadget.
- Ursula, the manipulative, evil, half-octopus sea witch from the movie *The Little Mermaid*.

Whoa, Nellie.

Here's what we discovered as Wen unpacked the rationale behind her admiration for these individuals: All three characters were strong, intellectual women (er . . . witches, half–sea creatures, whatever) who were independent, knowledgeable, resourceful, calculating, strategic, anything but passive, and who did things their own way and went after what they wanted.

Wow.

Minus the maniacal sorceress bit, that was also Wen — independent, resourceful, calculating, and strategic. But Wen struggled to be assertive, to do things her own way, and was often afraid to go after what she wanted. In fact, she was struggling to get her career moving in the right direction largely because of her passivity and her fear of taking bold action. Her inspirational figures had an amalgam of qualities — some she shared and was proud of, and some she *aspired* to.

This is the case for most of the people I work with. They find that the people who inspire them already share some of the qualities they have, and also hint at some of the qualities they desire that lie just beneath the surface, in gestation, waiting to bust out.

At first, thinking about the people who inspire you — real or fictional — might seem like the least career-relevant thing you could do. After all, you probably have no desire to become a rebel soldier fighting against the machine takeover, or a celebrity chef, or (hopefully) a maniacal cartoon villain.

But if you dig deeper to search for the qualities that all of your inspirational figures share, some themes will emerge. These are career clues — sometimes pointing in a specific career direction (like Pete), sometimes underscoring the personal qualities you want to flex in your career (like Hayley), or sometimes suggesting that there are both existing qualities that you want to flex, and also others that you want to develop and step into (like Wen).

So my question for you is: Who inspires you? Who do you admire? And, more importantly — why?

➽ DON'T FIGHT WHO YOU ARE ⬳

You're going to learn a lot about yourself over the course of this book. I hope that's already happening. So now seems like the right time to share some advice: Don't fight who you are. There are some deep, natural, inherent qualities that you have that are a big part of making you *you*. Don't go against your nature. I'm not saying abandon your attempts to grow or learn or evolve in new ways. I'm saying don't push down the qualities and quirks and desires that make you who you are. Don't betray yourself to become a copy of someone else just because you think it's the "right" thing to do.

Andi is a social butterfly. She loves meeting new people and bringing them together to share fun ideas and activities. She's bright, bubbly, chatty, and engaging. And she's warm, confident, and outspoken. People are drawn to her and follow her willingly. She's been that way for as long as she can remember. It's like it's coded right into her DNA. As a kid, Andi was often told that she was too loud, too social, too outspoken, and too bossy. (Side rant: The same qualities that get little girls called "bossy" get little boys called "leaders." Fuck that.)

After being told to tone it down again and again, young Andi came to see her bubbly, social, outspoken personality as a fault — something to overcome and suppress if she was to be accepted as a good girl.

Flash-forward about a decade and a half, and Andi is sitting across from me, a new graduate with an identity crisis, feeling unsure of who she is and how to show up in her career.

Keep in mind that Andi had spent the better part of 20 years in an educational system that typically punishes children

Don't push down
the qualities and
quirks and desires
that make you
who you are.

for being loud and chatty and outspoken and rewards them for being serious and subservient, and for following instead of leading. Andi learned how to fall in line, but that bubbly, social, outspoken little girl inside of her never really went away.

Part of Andi's problem was that she believed (falsely) that to be successful in any given career you had to get serious, follow the leaders, shut up, and conform. No wonder she was having an identity crisis and was feeling lost about where she could fit in. Her idea of what work had to be like went against her very nature.

So we spent some time getting reacquainted with Andi's suppressed younger self — that vibrant, bubbly, social little girl. She was still there and was *dying* to be let out of jail. We considered what kinds of careers that part of herself might enjoy. She landed on publicist. She'd get to meet new people all of the time and, more importantly, her buoyant, bubbly, social personality would actually be an *asset*, not a liability. She had two interviews for publicity jobs in the same week and landed them both, and is now happily killin' it in her job as a publicist, using her natural strengths.

Natalie is a law graduate who was deeply intuitive as a child, but she felt like the intuitive side of her was beat down in law school, in favor of her analytical side. She doesn't feel at all psyched about working in law as a result, and she feels divorced from her most natural self.

Lex is a creative visionary. He's been successful in the first few years of his career but never gets to use (or even discuss) any of his creative ideas. As a result, he's feeling empty and discouraged.

Samantha, on the other hand, is feeling great about her career. She was chastised for being nosy as a kid. She was wildly curious and was always digging into other people's business. She found a way to use that to her advantage and is working in marketing research, where digging into other people's business is a big part of the job.

Danielle is also someone who learned how to leverage her biggest, most natural strengths. She excels under pressure, especially time-based pressure, and loves the sink-or-swim nature of a big challenge. She thrives in chaos and loves being the calm in a crisis. So she loves her work planning and operating large events.

It's important to lean into and express your natural gifts (but, you know, only if you want to feel fulfilled in your work, so it's up to you). There are many, many ways for your gifts and talents to be expressed in your career, so get creative about how you could use them in a way that feels good to you. The more you acknowledge and honor who you really are, and the more you commit to using that stuff in your work, the happier your career will be.

> There are many, many ways for your gifts and talents to be expressed in your career.

But maybe you don't really feel like you know who you are or what your natural gifts are (which, BTW, is totally fine — we're just getting started). If so, I'd like to invite you to simply do the following . . .

→ GIVE A FUCK ←

What are the things you care about? Even if some of those things seem to have no fathomable connection to a career. (Spoiler alert: They do. You just haven't made the connection yet.) One of my clients was turned off by most careers except for those related to kids and the environment. Most other careers made her want to roll her eyes, but she genuinely gave a fuck about kids and the environment.

There are two main schools of thought when it comes to the idea of turning something you care about — a value or something you enjoy — into your career. And I'm going to ruin the surprise right now by telling you that neither of these schools of thought are absolutely right or wrong.

One school of thought basically says, *Hell yes!!! All passion all of the time!!! Follow your bliss!!! Do what you love and you'll never work a day in your life!!!* First of all, that's crazy. You're going to have an occasional shitty day even in your dream job. But also, you spend most of the waking hours of your life at work. Don't you want it to be something you enjoy and care about?

The second school of thought says, *Why in the actual*

depths of hell would you want to turn something you love into WORK?! That's too much pressure, and it's just going to ruin it for you. On the one hand, dang, what if doing that thing you love for eight hours a day turns it into a slog? But on the other hand, what if it doesn't, and it's fucking amazing?

This career stuff would be so much easier if there were a clear-cut rule you could follow to guarantee a slam dunk. Or if Judge Judy herself could show up at your house and sentence you to a lifetime of career bliss. Case dismissed.

The hard truth is you have to feel it out for yourself, which is about as unscientific a process as it gets. First, it helps to get familiar with the things you care about — your values, certain causes, and even specific activities and tasks that you could potentially integrate into your career. And then you have to ask yourself, *What might my life look like if I integrated this into my work in different ways?* Would it feel good? Again, there is no one right answer to this question. You have to feel it out. Here's how some of my clients did it:

Matt went to graphic design school and had a lot of success with that early in his career. But there were other things he longed to do — cooking, for one, and acting, for another. He had thought about those two things for years but wasn't sure if he should pull the trigger and make a career change.

In his case, he decided not to. (Someone else in the same situation might have made the opposite choice, and that would have been fine, too. These decisions are personal and subjective.) What Matt *did* decide to do was to make more room for both of those things — cooking and acting — in his life. He took a cooking class and devoted more time to making food, and he researched community theatres and acting classes so he could nurture that part of himself, too, which he hadn't really done since he was a kid.

You may choose to do this, too. If there are interests you have and parts of yourself that you care about deeply but don't envision as a good fit for your career, please find a way to make them a part of your *life*. And be sure to choose a career that actually supports your intention to have those things in your life, not one that limits your ability to do so.

> The hard truth is you have to feel it out for yourself, which is about as unscientific a process as it gets.

And at the very least, be sure to pursue work that doesn't go *against* your values. Caden studied ecology and environmental science, and after graduation he noticed that many of his peers were getting jobs with oil excavation companies working in tar sands. That went deeply against his values (again, a personal and subjective thing), and so he pursued career options that were very different from many of his former classmates.

Shawn has a chemical engineering degree. He has a brilliant analytical mind and is in many ways very well suited to engineering. But the further he moved into his chemical engineering career, the more he realized something was missing. Shawn cares deeply about the environment. He spends nearly all of his time outdoors, cycling and climbing. He cares about environmental sustainability and keenly follows advances in sustainability, reading constantly about things like clean technology. It's an obsession of his. After digging deep and getting more familiar with his values and priorities, he realized that he wanted to integrate those things more into his work. So Shawn decided to shift his career in the direction of environmental engineering and clean tech. Integrating something he deeply cared about into his career felt essential for Shawn, and in his case it was a small shift that has made a *big* difference in how he feels about his career. Sometimes that's all it takes.

➠ YOUR SECRET WEAPON: INFORMATIONAL INTERVIEWS ⬅

It's hard to run with an idea you have about what you might want to do for your career. Because an idea is just, well, an idea. And you're never totally sure if you've got it right. Is your idea well informed or is it just some kind of fantasy? I mean, those chicks you follow on Instagram sure seem to be livin' the dream, but their careers can't be *that* good can they? You know no job is perfect, and you'd rather know the good, the bad, and the ugly before you make your move.

Basically, you want to make sure your *idea* of what a certain career is going to be like is what it's *actually* like.

We're going to do that with informational interviews. Have you heard of them? A lot of people haven't. They're like an insider secret and, let me tell you, they're like a secret weapon when it comes to creating a feel-good career.

Maybe the word "interview" makes you shudder. If so, every time you see the words "informational interview," I want you to just think *coffee with cool people who you want to learn stuff from*. Because that's exactly what informational interviews are — they're just coffee with cool people. People you want to learn career stuff from.

Let's say you went to school for international development, but you have a hunch you'd rather work in communications. But you don't have a damn clue how to make that transition.

Or maybe you have a Bachelor of Commerce. But you know there are a gazillion things you could do with that and you're not sure what's right for you. Or even what your options are.

Or what if you started a career in event management, but you think you might be happier doing something that's somehow related to holistic wellness? That's a pretty radical shift. Feels kinda daunting.

Enter the informational interview.

Talking to real people doing real work in an area you think you might be interested in (or one you're not even *sure* about because you know so little about it) is the best way to get good information. It's better than classes or books or Googling your ass off (though those things can be helpful, too). Talking to *real* people about *real* work gets you *real* information — the kind of information you need before you can make a decision.

If you went to school for international development, but you think you'd rather work in communications, you'll want to talk to a lot of people working in communications to see where you might fit in.

If you have a Bachelor of Commerce but no idea what to do with it, you'll want to talk to movers and shakers in the business world — maybe even alumni from your school to see what exciting things are out there.

If you're not diggin' your event management career and would rather be working in holistic wellness, you'll want to learn about the many different kinds of holistic wellness work and what that work entails before you make the jump, right?

BTW, if you think these examples are random, they're not. Clients of mine made these exact transitions. All with the help of informational interviews.

These people started out feeling totally clueless. Until they started to gather information. They gathered some basic stuff from the internet, but they quickly moved on to talk to people IRL to fill their information gaps.

Yeah, but how do I do that?

Glad you asked! First, you figure out what your information gaps are — in other words, what info you need before you can make a decision. You'll find some of that on the interwebs, but mostly you want to find people who you think might have that information. And then you ask to talk to them. That's it. (And you don't have to know exactly which direction you want to take your career in to do this. If there are a few careers you're considering, explore all of them with informational interviews. The whole point is to gather good information, so you can narrow things down.)

Start by making a mental list of the stuff you want to know, the things that would help you make your decision. If you had a knowledgeable, benevolent unicorn of a human being sitting across from you over a cup of coffee, what questions would you ask?

These questions might include general questions like: *What is your typical day like? What do you like/dislike about your job? How did you come to work in this field?* You should probably include lots of specific questions about the things that matter to you. For example, based on what we learned about my own work preferences in the last couple of chapters, here are some questions I'd ask because they're directly related to the stuff I personally care about and would need to know to make a good career decision:

- How closely do you work with your colleagues/clients?
- How much autonomy do you have in your work?
- What kind of problems do you help people with?
- Do you work on projects for a long stretch of time or switch tasks frequently?
- Is research or statistics a big part of your job?
- Do you get to teach or mentor much in your work?

And the list goes on.

I'd also ask them if there's anything they'd like to share that I haven't asked about. (Just in case there's something important I've overlooked.) And if there's anyone else they think I should talk to. (Because that might get me some great leads!) And then I'd thank them for their time and then go home and scribble notes like a mofo, so I wouldn't forget anything.

By the way, this isn't some bullshit hypothetical "best practices" thing I'm asking you to do but would never do myself. I've done this. Lots of times. I *still* do this, years into my career. Before I went to grad school, I reached out to a bunch of professors and students in a bunch of graduate programs. I asked them what it was like, what to expect, what they liked about it, what they didn't, what the workload was like — everything I could think of.

When I wanted to write for big publications like *Forbes* and *Inc.* and *Entrepreneur* (with no portfolio and no idea what the hell I was doing), I reached out to journalists and contributors to figure that shit out. I asked embarrassingly basic questions like, *So what is a pitch, exactly? Who do you send it to? Should I do this over email? Keep it short, or longer with elaboration? Include writing samples?* Let's not forget I had a journalism degree. I should have known that stuff, but I didn't. So I had to ask.

Before I wrote my first book, I reached out to other authors — all of them total strangers. How else was I gonna do it? Who the hell just knows how to write a book? I didn't. In every case — with grad school, getting published, writing a book, making a career change — I did as much research as I could on my own and then reached out to a bunch of strangers I thought could help. Many of them said no (or didn't even get back to me), some of them said yes, some of them were helpful, and some of them were not. And it was worth it. EVERY. TIME.

➡ HOW TO ASK FOR AN INFORMATIONAL INTERVIEW ⬅

Given the information you want to gather, think of some of the people who might be able to provide some of the information you need. You'll want to start with people you know or people you can have someone introduce you to, but those connections will run out very quickly, so you'll have to do your research (on LinkedIn, company websites, or anywhere really) to find some cool people to approach on your own.

I should warn you that rejection is a regular part of informational interviews. People are busy. Only one out of every four or five people you approach will be down for getting together with you, and the rest of the time you'll hear crickets (if so, send a follow-up request a week later), or people will say they're too busy. It's not personal, so don't get all weird about it. Just send out your slew of requests and see what comes back.

Okay, so I know what questions I have, and an idea of who I'd like to talk to, but how do I get this person to have coffee with me?

You just ask.

Really?

Yup. You ask. The people you ask might be people you know or total strangers. Here's what asking might look like:

Subject: Interested in your work

From: You

To: coolperson@letschat.com

Hi _____,

I'm a _____ (your degree) grad and I'm currently working _____ (say what kind of work you're doing now). I'm hoping to eventually develop my career in the area of _____, specifically _____. I'm not looking for a job or connection, but I'm very interested in learning more about your field of work, and especially your own experience with _____ (say their industry or something they're working on). Would you be willing to chat? Coffee is on me, and of course I'm happy to work around your schedule at whatever location is best for you. Let me know what you think.

Sincerely,
Your Name

BOOM. That's what a winning informational interview request looks like.

I want you to notice three important things here:

1. *You're not telling the person your life story.* Why? They're busy. Also, they don't care because they don't know you yet.
2. *You're making it clear that you're not asking for a job.* You're just looking for information about their work. (Which is way less icky than asking a total stranger for a job hookup. Ew.)
3. *You're making it easy for them to say yes* by keeping your email short and offering to work around their schedule and location.

Side note: If you don't know exactly what kind of work you want to do, no problemo. Just say that. Or if you're not working, just say that. Or if you're still a student, just say that. Perhaps you're noticing that the point isn't to impress the person you're meeting with; it's to gather information.

Now you know what information you need, who to ask, and how to ask for it. You're on your way! With all these coffee chats, you're about to be super caffeinated and also way more knowledgeable than before. WIN.

> ## The point isn't to impress the person you're meeting with; it's to gather information.

Listen, it's quite possible that the idea of actually reaching out to people for informational interviews makes you want to anxiety puke (*raises hand*). But at the risk of sounding naggy, please, please, PLEASE actually follow through on this. Talking to real people in order to get real information (despite the awkwardness of approaching strangers and the inevitability of some rejection) is probably the single most helpful thing I've ever done as I've navigated my career. My clients say it's made all the difference for them, too. Sure, you could white-knuckle it along through the rapids of your career, but the journey will be way less freaky with an experienced guide or two to show you the way.

4

THE BURDEN OF TRUTH

You probably have one or two ideas about what might make you happy in your career — even if those ideas still seem half-baked or vague as fuck. Here's what most people do when they get those vague inklings: They shut them down. They let their fear and frustration get the best of them. When the right career path doesn't seem obvious or easy right away, they throw their hands up and say . . .

*Welp. I haven't got a clue. I guess I'll just
do what my dad tells me to do.*

OR

This is too hard. Maybe I'll just stick
with this shit job I already have.

OR

Jesus, the thing I want to do is reeeeeally different than
what I'm doing now. Never mind. Impossible.

Do you know why most people do this? Why people give up the hunt just as they're about to get on a hot track? Because knowing what you want can be really scary. It comes with pressure. Admitting what you want puts you in a tricky position. You either have to get after what you want or give up on yourself. Most people prefer the guise of ignorance to the burden of truth. Because when you know the truth about what you want, you have to *do* something about it.

Most people prefer the guise of ignorance to the burden of truth.

And if you don't know exactly *what* to do or where to start, you've got a brand new problem. The problem shifts from *I don't know what I want* to *I don't know how to have what I want.*

That's why people fold and head for the hills just as they're getting really close to figuring things out. The truth about what they want feels impossible and scares the shit out of them, so they shut it down, saying, *But I can't do THAT!*

Maybe the inklings and whispers about what you want for your career have you saying stuff like:

But I didn't go to school for that!

OR

But that wasn't a part of the plan!

OR

But I don't have any experience with that!

OR

But I don't know how to get that!

Here's the good news: None of that stuff has to stop you from moving forward.

⇒ THE ORIGINAL PLAN ⇐

There's a good chance that what you want wasn't a part of the Original Plan.

The Original Plan was to know exactly what you wanted, with unwavering clarity, as a 17-year-old kid in high school, then go to school for that thing, graduate with a slew of super badass job offers from people dying to hire you for that thing, pick the best one, and then spend the rest of your life living happily ever after doing that thing. THE END.

Yeah. How often do you think that works out for people?

Never, dude. Like, zero. Finding a career you love always takes way more work than a fairy tale. And way more contingency plans than you'd like.

But WHY?!

It's because you're human. And there's no changing that. (The science just isn't there yet.) We humans tend to change and evolve and grow as we get older. Pesky little detail, isn't it? That's why the Original Plan — whatever career path you were forced to choose as a hormonal, rapidly changing human of 17 years — might not feel like it hits the mark anymore. You've changed a lot since then.

Let me guess: When you were five years old, you wanted to be a doctor or a teacher or a veterinarian when you grew up. Your sweet little five-year-old self was pretty clueless about all of the options out there, so those careers seemed like a good way to go. You had been to the doctor. You had a teacher. You knew these jobs existed. Also, dogs are cool. Hence every five-year-old's career wish list.

But then you grew as a person, learned a little bit more about life, and reconsidered your options. That's what you did in high school and college, and that may be what you're doing again now. And spoiler alert: That's what you'll *continue* to do until the day you die. Which is why the career you choose to do now might not be the career you choose to do 5 or 10 or 20 years from now.

breathing into paper bag

I know, I know. STRESSFUL, right?! That's life, man. Pretending it isn't so isn't going to help you; you might as well face it now. You're a changeable, growing human. The only way to get out of that contract is death, so I guess it's not so bad after all, right?

Your inner control freak hates this constant change thing. I know mine does. Everybody wants to graduate from school, clap their hands together, and say, *Whew, now that I've put in all that work I guess I can just follow the yellow brick road to success and fulfillment. Where are my ruby slippers, anyway?* Instead, a lot of people get out of school and panic because they start noticing that what they want *now* isn't the same as what they wanted back *then*. Gulp.

This is more common than you might think. Only 7% of 25-year-olds have the same career goals as they did when they were 17. (Which you might remember is exactly when you had to choose your educational path. Oy.) That means that 93% of people who are at the beginning of their careers are going, *Wait. What? I had this plan and it doesn't feel good anymore. Fuuuuuck.* That's the norm, not the exception. Now, just because it's the norm doesn't mean it isn't also stressful.

I graduated from my undergrad with two things: a Bachelor of Journalism and a strong desire *not* to work as a journalist. CUE THE PANIC. I didn't see that coming back when I'd applied to school. But there I was with a shiny new degree and no plan. Sticking to my Original Plan would have meant pursuing a career I knew I'd hate, so even though my inner control freak haaaaated the idea of winging it and coming up with a new plan, it's what I had to do. (You know, if I wanted to actually *enjoy* my life.)

A potential departure from the Original Plan is a little easier to digest when you look back at all of the other times you moved on from the Original Plan. Because you've already done that lots of times. Any time you've ever changed your mind or tried something different, you let go of the Original Plan — like if you went to a school you hadn't originally considered, or if you moved in with a new roommate, or if you dropped a class and took something different, or if you realized that the shirt you planned to wear this morning was in the laundry, so you put on something else. Plan B. Not so bad, right?

You'll have to ditch the Original Plan if you went to school for something you don't actually enjoy (like me with journalism school), or if you take a job that *sounded* awesome but actually *feels* shitty once you start, or if you find yourself living in a city you hate, or if you're in a relationship that isn't working. There are approximately one hundred gazillion things that might force you off a path you thought you were going to stay on. A client of mine went to school for rec and leisure, but it turned out not to be at all what she wanted. So she had to ditch her Original Plan. Another client tried doing freelance work in an area he loved, but he couldn't make enough money to support himself. So he had to ditch his Original Plan. Another client hated living in the city and uprooted her entire life, including her home, her job, and her relationships, to go live in the woods. Talk about ditching your Original Plan.

Ditching the Original Plan is often (almost always, actually) going to be a part of your career journey. And as stressful as it may seem, change is a really good thing because it keeps you moving in a direction that feels good. So go ahead and make some plans, but don't clutch them too tightly. What you want will change over time, so you have to roll with it. Be flexible, be open, and know that changing your mind just means you're growing and paying attention and following what matters to you.

> Go ahead and make some plans,
> but don't clutch them too tightly.

FALSE START

It's one thing to graduate from school and immediately realize you want to start a career in a different direction. It's another thing to get out of school, bust your ass building a career for a year or two (or five or ten), and *then* realize that you're in the wrong career. That'll give a person a full-blown panic attack. You'll want to just cash in your chips, say your goodbyes, overfeed your cat, and climb into the nearest shark tank.

You'll wonder, *How in the name of Chris Hemsworth did this happen?! Did I just get punked? What am I supposed to do now?* You slaved away in school, racked up debt, finally graduated, and hustled away building a career, all the while wondering, *Goddammit, Universe, could you make this any HARDER?*

Universe: *Hold my beer.*

When you discover you're on the wrong career path, your first reaction will probably be denial. You'll think, *You know what? Everything is FINE. I'm actually FINE. It's FINE.* Until it's not fine. Until that twisty, churning feeling in the pit of your stomach gets so strong that you can't ignore it anymore, and you have to actually *do* something about it.

Reinvention is possible. Listen, it's not a cakewalk, but it's certainly possible. And it's possible for you. People do it all the time. And the good news is it's actually easier to reinvent yourself near the *beginning* of your career than it is 30 years in. If you have a false start, you can start again.

Shane is someone who did just that. He busted his ass at law school and snagged a gig as a law associate after graduation. But things quickly unraveled from there. He realized that the life of a lawyer was not for him, but he felt panicked about changing careers after putting in all of that work. Plus, he was terrified about what people would think of him if he left a prestigious field like law for something else. Despite his fear, Shane was willing to explore his desires. He liked fashion and design but not enough to make a career of it. He also loved sports and athletics. He considered becoming a personal trainer for athletes or working in sport event management. The idea of supporting elite, world-class athletes in some way was really exciting to Shane, but also couldn't have been further from his life as a lawyer. It turns out that a radical change was exactly what he needed. Shane is now a senior manager at a national sport organization, creating programming for Olympic-level athletes.

> *Goddammit, Universe, could you make this any HARDER?*
> *Universe: Hold my beer.*

Now *that* is reinvention. *Radical* reinvention.

Another client of mine, Perrin, also started her career as a corporate lawyer. (No shade to the law profession, but I work with a lot of lawyers dying to get out.) Perrin felt lucky to have snagged a job at a good firm right after school. She liked her colleagues. And the work culture at her firm was actually good. The hours weren't unreasonable, and the pace of the work wasn't overwhelming, which definitely wasn't the case for most of her former classmates working at other law firms. She could actually have a *life* outside of work.

But something didn't feel right. In her gut, Perrin knew

she wasn't meant to be a lawyer. But she had been raised by a family that taught her that prestigious professions like law and medicine and a small handful of others were the only respectable options for careers. Perrin was smart and hard-working and had thought that law might be an okay fit, given the limited "acceptable" options. So she had applied for law school, was accepted, worked hard, graduated, and started her career. She was doing everything "right." But there was a churning feeling in the pit of her stomach, and that churning feeling said, *I do not want to be a lawyer.* When she listened closer, it also said, *I want to be a nutritionist.*

Hoo boy.

What is WRONG with me?! Perrin thought. *I've worked so hard for this. Shouldn't I be happy with what I have?*

Imagine you go out for lunch on a cold, rainy day. While you're on the way to the restaurant you think, *Damn, I sure could cozy up with a nice bowl of soup today. I think that's what I'll get.* When you arrive, your server informs you that the soup of the day is clam chowder. Unfortunately, you don't like clam chowder. So you tell your server you'll need a few more minutes with the menu to pick something else.

"Yes, but this is *very good* clam chowder," the server says.

"I'm sure it is," you say. "But I don't like clam chowder."

As you're looking over the menu, the server brings you a bowl of clam chowder. And also one for everyone else at the table.

"I'm sorry," you say. "I don't like clam chowder."

"I don't understand," says the server. "This is a five-star

fine dining establishment run by one of the world's finest chefs. He makes an excellent chowder."

"Just eat it!" your lunch companions say encouragingly. "It really is superb. We love it."

But just looking at that goddamn clam chowder makes your stomach churn.

That's what it's like when you say to yourself, *Shouldn't I be happy with what I have? Shouldn't I just suck it up and eat this clam chowder?*

Sure, maybe you could choke it down once or twice, but when the clam chowder is your *career*, we're talking about serving it up every day for the rest of your life. Not a tasty option.

My point: Don't spend your life eating clam chowder if you don't like clam chowder. Order something else.

I have a client who was trained as a registered immigration consultant and is now a yogi and meditation instructor. Another who used to work in the hospitality industry and is now a makeup artist. One who was a college admissions officer and became a life coach. And another who ditched her career in public relations to become an accountant. (And you'll be happy to hear that Perrin, the lawyer, is now on her way to becoming a nutritionist.)

Yeah, but changes like that are for insanely brave people, you might think. *Or for people who have a crapload of cash. Or a really amazing support system.*

Not so.

All of the people mentioned here were absolutely terrified

before making these changes. And none of them were swimming in cash (in fact, many still had student debt). And several of them had families and friends who were . . . shall we say . . . not huge supporters. And they did it anyway.

Now, not everyone needs to make a radical 180-degree turn to get happier at work. For some people, a small change of direction can make a *big* difference. People like Aiden.

Aiden has an acting and vocal performance degree. He's been creating and performing shows since he was a child. But in the process of exploring his interests, Aiden discovered that what he loves most about performance isn't actually the *performance* part at all; it's the behind-the-scenes collaborative work of making something with a group of creative people — figuring out how all of the moving pieces can come together to make something that will entertain people.

With this new knowledge, Aiden decided to change direction and move into television *production* — to focus on the kind of behind-the-scenes collaborative work that he's loved all along. He's not yet sure how he wants to specialize. Reality TV? Dramas? Commercial music videos? Pop culture and news with a company like Vice? He's keeping his options open. In the meantime, he's scored his first gig as a production coordinator for a TV show and is learning a ton on the job. It was a relatively small shift. He's still working in the entertainment industry, and still specifically in television, but it was a change in direction that feels like a better fit.

Another client of mine, Grace, made an even smaller shift. She was a nurse who came to me and was seriously considering leaving the field of nursing entirely. Her main problem was that the hospital she worked for had a toxic, gossipy, back-stabby work culture. *This is what it must be like to work as a nurse*, she thought. But the problem wasn't the field of nursing at all; it was her employer. No need to reinvent the wheel or throw the baby out with the bathwater — she just needed to work at a different hospital.

It was the same for Laura, an executive assistant who worked for a team of condescending assholes. She didn't even have to change employers; she just had to transfer to a different team. And Mona, who started a career in human resources, found that she didn't like implementing and supporting H.R. policies, but she did like *teaching* H.R. So much so that she's teaching H.R. full time now and getting her master's in education — a small but significant shift. Change comes in all shapes and sizes. How big a change you make — a total 180, or a little 10-degree pivot — is entirely up to you.

➡ THE FEEL-GOOD ZONE ⬅

I want to talk to you about stepping into what I call the *feel-good zone* — moving toward work that feels good mentally, emotionally, and even physically.

Physically?

Yes, physically.

Really?

Yup. Here's what I mean . . .

Have you ever worked on a project or done an activity where you felt fully engaged, so much so that you lost track of time and felt totally in the zone? Something that made you feel awake and energized and more alive? Where you felt on fire and inspired, like there was an electric current flowing right through you?

That's what I'm talking about. That's what feel-good work should feel like, physically. Not all day, every day, obviously (no job is perfect), but most of the time. After all, we spend half of our waking lives at work. Don't you want it to feel good?

The feel-good zone feels slightly different for everybody. Some people say they feel free. Others say they feel highly focused and engaged. Many say they feel more alert and alive. When I'm in my feel-good zone, I feel super focused and energized, like I bumped up my voltage by an extra 20%. *Zap!* I feel unstoppable. I feel like this when I work with my clients or write or give a keynote talk. Those are things I feel like I'm *meant* to do, so I feel super charged when I do them. For you, maybe it's when you design something beautiful, or solve a really tricky technical problem, or help someone feel better, or spend time with artists, or any number of things.

Think of a project or activity that made you feel really good. And not sex. That's not a career option. (Okay, technically it is, but let's not go there.)

Now, what did that thing feel like *physically* for you? Did you feel lighter? More awake? Like you were buzzing? In other words, what does your feel-good zone feel like, *physically?* How would you describe how it feels?

One of my clients gets an excited, bubbly sensation in his stomach when he's in the feel-good zone. Like a fizzy, effervescent carbonated feeling. And when he's way outside of his feel-good zone he feels a gnarled, twisty knot in the pit of his stomach, like something heavy is weighing him down.

We spend half of our waking lives at work. Don't you want it to feel good?

Another client noticed that she feels more open and expansive and free when she's in the feel-good zone. And when she's not, she feels constrained and trapped and small.

This is an especially powerful thing to think about if you're still feeling slightly fuzzy about which career you want to pursue. Or even if you know where you want to go, but not which path you want to take to get there.

Your feel-good zone is something you'll want to look for, or rather *feel* for, as you navigate your career. Did you ever play that hot/cold game when you were a kid? The one where you had to find something with your eyes closed and the only clues you got were warmer (you're getting closer) and colder (oops, wrong way)? Paying attention to when you're in the feel-good career zone (getting warmer) and when you're not (oops, wrong way) will always help point you in the right direction in your career (and in life, too, for that matter).

Have you ever had a conversation with a friend about something they're trying to be happy about, but you can tell they're just not into it? Like maybe a friend who is talking about all the crap she has to do because she's somebody's bridesmaid. She's trying to seem happy and gracious and excited about all of it, but her smile is cracking a little and she actually seems exhausted. Or maybe a friend who's in a bad relationship but reeeeeally doesn't want to admit the truth. He's wearing a smile, but his eyes are dead, and he seems kind of mopey and detached.

You can see right through that shit. You know your bridesmaid friend is stressed and overwhelmed. You know your friend is miserable in his relationship. You know because it's written on their faces. Our bodies tell us so much. About each other, and (if we pay attention) about ourselves.

Consider a couple of the career options you're thinking about for a moment, whether it's a few totally different careers or one career with different paths to get there. For example, maybe you're considering becoming a copywriter, or journalist, or a content manager. Or you might really want to get into international relations, but you're not sure which path to take, so you're considering a NATO internship, federal foreign services, or maybe working with the Red Cross.

Hold each of your ideas individually in your mind. How do you feel, physically, when you think about working as a copywriter? A journalist? A content manager? Or whatever it is you're considering. Some of the options you're considering might make you feel better than others — warmer, lighter, freer, more energetic. Use that information to help you make feel-good career decisions. It will always steer you in the right direction.

➡ HELL YES FEAR VS. HELL NO FEAR ⬅

Now here's a potential complication: What if the stuff you really want to do makes your stomach flip-flop because it feels scary? And you can't really tell if that flip-flop feeling is a good thing or a bad thing?

Thinking about going after some of the things you want probably has you shaking in your boots. That's totally normal. In fact, it might actually be an indication that you're moving in the right direction. When we really want something, the stakes feel high, and our fear skyrockets. Maybe that's exactly how you're feeling now.

But how can you tell if the fear you're feeling is that exciting, deep-breath, take-the-plunge kind of fear, or the kind of fear that feels like aversion, like you're wading into yucky waters?

Here's the difference: When you really, truly want something, the kind of fear you usually feel is what I call *hell yes* fear. It's a good kind of scary because it's also exciting at the same time. It feels like fear plus anticipation. But when you're facing something you think you *have* to do (like, maybe whatever a parent thinks you should do for your career), you may feel what I call *hell no* fear. It's a repulsive kind of fear. It feels like fear plus aversion.

Will is a client of mine. For as long as he can remember, he's wanted to be a firefighter — and not in the cutesy way that little boys want to be firefighters so they can play the hero, wear the cool hat, and ride in the big truck. Will was *legit* obsessed with firefighting as a real profession. He had done the research to learn about training and hiring practices and job progression. He weighed the benefits and drawbacks on health and lifestyle. He had friends who were firefighters, and he was always trying to meet more people in the fire community. He knew what the job entailed — including the exciting bits and the mundane bits — and what the day-to-day life of a firefighter was like. He knew the good, the bad, and the ugly, and he was still obsessed.

But the idea of actually *becoming* a firefighter was frightening to Will, and not for the reason you might expect. His fear had nothing to do with running into burning buildings or rushing to the scene of a severe car accident, where life and death are decided in a matter of minutes. He was fine with that. The adrenaline surge from such urgent, high-stakes work was actually part of the appeal. He was afraid of the same thing that *most* of us are afraid of in our careers: Uncertainty. The possibility of failure.

He wondered, *What if I actually go for it and fail? What if I go to fire school, get certified, but then never get hired? It's not like those jobs grow on trees. There aren't zillions of them, and they aren't exactly easy to get.*

Will was excited by the idea of being a firefighter — it was the life he could most easily envision for himself, and the thought of living that life energized him — but he was also afraid of trying and failing. His fear was of the *hell yes* variety.

What if I actually go for it and fail?

Hell yes fear isn't less scary than *hell no* fear. In fact, *hell yes* fear is often more frightening. When you feel kind of ambivalent about something, the prospect of failure isn't all that threatening. But the thought of taking a risk and going after the thing your heart most wants with the very real possibility of failure? That's *devastating*.

This is the part where I tell you that Will battled his demons, got brave, and *went for it*, right?

Actually, Will's fear got the best of him. *Maybe I should do something more traditional*, he thought. *Maybe this firefighter thing is a pipe dream. Maybe I should do something more practical.* And so, shortly after completing his undergraduate degree, Will found himself enrolled in physiotherapy school. He liked the idea of helping people. Plus, the work would be both mental and physical — a combo that mattered to him. Becoming a physiotherapist seemed like a safe bet.

But just a few months into his studies, Will started to feel like something wasn't right. He felt blah, like he had no pulse, which was really unlike him, and his "something doesn't feel right" feeling just kept getting stronger and stronger. That's when he reached out to me. He wanted some help to figure out WTF was going on.

It wasn't long until we discovered that Will was feeling some *hell no* fear (which often feels like lethargy and exhaustion) related to becoming a physiotherapist. He couldn't shake the thought of becoming a firefighter, but he was afraid to leave this new, safer, more practical path to take a risk on that. He was afraid to make a change, but he also couldn't muster any energy for this new physiotherapist path he had chosen. It was fear paired with aversion, and it was sapping his energy. He felt deflated, like a slow leak in an old balloon.

Sometimes you have to suffer through that *hell no* feeling (the heavy suck of *ugh*) for a while before you're willing to confront your fear and take a chance on *hell yes*. In other words, sometimes you have to know what the wrong choice feels like before you can find the strength to make the right one. Nobody knows this more than Will.

And NOW is the part of the story where I tell you that he got brave and went for it. (Sorry about the earlier psych-out!) Because Will never did return to physiotherapy school and is instead well on his way to becoming a firefighter.

Hell no fear vs. *hell yes* fear often boils down to safe but dull vs. scary but exciting. When you're going for something and you feel that scary but exciting *hell yes* feeling, you think, *Holy shit, am I actually going to do this?!* And then you activate your steely resolve and take a deep, bracing breath. When you're feeling the safe but dull feeling of *hell no*, you think, *Jesus Christ, I could nap for a decade.* The feeling can range from an apathetic *meh* to a strong, repugnant *DO NOT WANT.*

> Sometimes you have to know what the wrong choice feels like before you can find the strength to make the right one.

Consider Tom, who was afraid to quit his job selling cars so he could do what he really wanted — become a writer and speaker. Or Bri, who was afraid to leave her job as a landscape designer for a respectable company to break off and start her own business designing unconventional, avant-garde landscapes that nobody else was doing. Or Gabi, who was afraid to take a radical approach to her personal training business. She yearned to work as a recovery coach, using personal training to help recovering cocaine addicts reclaim their lives. That's not exactly a traditional career.

Each of these people felt the difference between being lovingly pulled in one direction (*hell yes*) vs. pushing themselves down a safe but dull path they didn't really want to be on (*hell no*). And luckily, they all found the mental and emotional strength to turn away from *hell no* toward *hell yes*. That's how you build a happy life. You won't be free from fear or uncertainty, but then again, comfort is highly overrated.

But even if you recognize your fear as the *hell yes* variety, and even if you desperately want to go for it, there's still the elephant in the room — that one lingering, nagging, but totally legit question: *What if I fail?*

You will.

Wait. WHAT?!

Not the crash and burn kind of fail. Just the *oops* kind. And maybe even the *oh shit* kind. It'll happen. Occasionally. And then you'll pick yourself up, dust yourself off, and keep going. No biggie. It's the *keep going* part that matters.

At various points in my career I've fucked up, picked the wrong thing, been fired, fallen apart, struggled, drudged through, and felt uncertain, stagnated, and utterly lost. And while I'm in a good place now, I'm not naïve enough to think that those days are over for me. Failures and fuckups and wrong turns are a part of being human.

That's how I'd like you to frame your own inevitable failures and fuckups and wrong turns, too: They're just a part of your humanity. You'll feel shitty for a while when things don't go as you'd hoped or intended, but then you'll lick your wounds and keep on truckin'.

And hell, you might actually have smashing success with a lot of your career goals. You might knock it out of the park on your very first time up to bat. It might feel like champagne and fireworks! Might be worth a try, right?

But if you don't hit all of your career goals right on the mark right away, that's okay. It's like that famous saying: *Shoot for the moon. Even if you miss, you'll land among some*

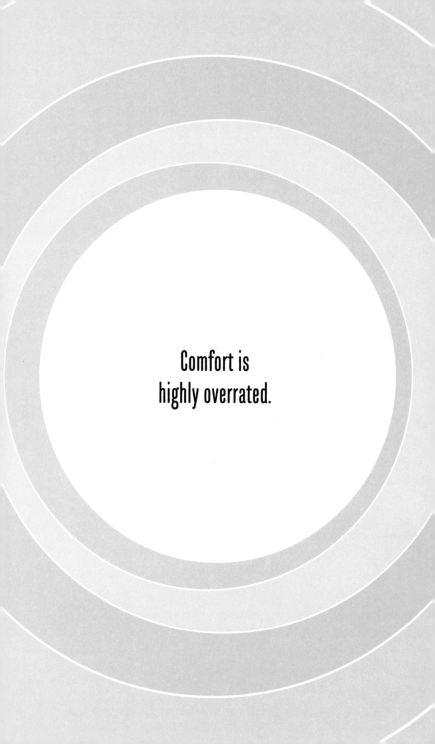

Comfort is
highly overrated.

other really cool career opportunities. Or something like that. Don't quote me.

Most things worth doing require a little bit of risk — you have to put yourself out there without really knowing what will happen. What might be worth the risk? Only you know.

➡➡ THE PATH OF LEAST RESISTANCE ⬅⬅

There's a question that's worth asking yourself early in your career: *Was this career path something I actually chose, or did I just end up here?* Sometimes people take the path of least resistance because, well, less resistance is kind of appealing. Unfortunately, the easiest path isn't always the best one.

Jen has degrees in politics and history, but somehow she just kind of fell into software sales. "I know that's crazy," she said. "But it just kind of . . . happened." It turns out that Jen is actually *really good* at software sales, but she doesn't care about it. It's not what she wanted.

Similarly, Mary is a project manager at a bank. She ended up there because a family member said she had a hookup for a job. But Mary actually wants to work in public health.

This brings us to another important question: *Did I choose this career path, or did someone else choose it for me?*

Mary felt sick about leaving her job at the bank. Her family member had stuck her neck out for her, and she didn't want to seem ungrateful. She *was* grateful. So grateful! At the time, she was out of school and didn't have work yet, it had felt like exactly what she needed. But not anymore. It wasn't a conscious choice she'd made for her long-term future. It had just sort of . . . happened. Yes, she'd *let* it happen, and at the time even *wanted* it to happen. But only because it was the path of least resistance.

Taking the path of least resistance isn't always a bad thing. There's nothing wrong with trying something out to see how it feels. Jen might have loved working in sales. Mary actually *did* enjoy her project management job at the bank for a while. If you love where you land, by all means, OWN IT. Everyone should be so lucky. But if you don't love where you land, you need to make a change.

The easiest path isn't always the best one.

Landing in the wrong career because it was the path of least resistance is a common thing. Especially when you got there on the advice of some kind of expert, or with encouragement from someone you love and trust. In fact, it makes a lot of sense if this is what happened to you. Why? Because for the last two decades you've made most of your decisions based on other people's advice. Sure, you made some choices on your own, but your mom or dad or teachers or mentors were always there to steer you in the "right" direction.

One of my clients — I'll call her Ava — had a lot of anxiety about navigating her career. She said, "I've never had to make my own decisions before." I think that's true for a lot of people in their 20s.

If someone (like, oh, say, your mom) has been co-piloting your life up until now, you may feel totally freaked out about taking control and flying solo. As in, *But I don't know what I'm doing!* As in, *But my mom and dad want me to do this other thing instead!* As in, *But I'm afraid I'll fuck things up and crash in a horrible fiery death!*

You won't. Oh, you'll definitely make some mistakes along the way, just like every other person who ever lived, but you'll be just fine.

Or maybe it's not a parent who's co-piloting your life. Maybe it's a team of real or imaginary "experts." Experts. You know, like your high-school guidance counselor. Or that super scientific personality assessment you did. Or that article you read from the *New York Times*. Or that fancy aptitude test you took.

If you're betting your future on anything — from news articles to sophisticated assessments to the latest Buzzfeed quiz — just stop. Don't let a quiz or a survey or a counselor or even a parent tell you what to do.

When you're freaked out and unsure, it seems easier to look outside of yourself for answers. There's a reason why everyone goes to see their college career counselor at the eleventh hour, right before graduation. It's because people panic and think, *Jesus, I don't know what the hell I'm doing, so I better just ASK someone.* There's so much pressure to get it right. Plus, if you outsource your decision-making, you don't *really* have to take responsibility for the choices you make, right? You were just doing what you were told. (Bullshit. That's a cop-out.)

Here's the truth: The biggest expert on you is (big surprise) *you*. Not me or some other "expert," or the internet, or a guidance counselor, or even your mom or dad. It's you.

The people who love you, along with the experts and authorities you consult, will all have opinions about what you should do with your life. Hell, a lot of the opinions flying around you might even be totally unsolicited. You know the joke: Opinions are like assholes — everybody's got one.

Maybe your bestie thinks you should work for the same company as her, so you can have lunch together every day. It sounds okay. And easy because she can hook you up. But you're not really psyched about the work. Or maybe your dad thinks you should go to law school. After all, you're a smart cookie. And lawyers make lots of money, don't they? But something about it doesn't feel quite right. Or maybe one of your college professors thinks you should stay on as her research assistant and do your master's. That's super flattering, but there are other things you want to try.

Some of the opinions flying at you might seem helpful. And some of them might just seem like noise. The truth is that when it comes to your career, there's no such thing as objectively good or bad advice. Good advice is simply advice that feels good and seems true to *you*. And bad advice is simply advice that turns you off, the stuff that feels like noise to *you*. When you get advice from the people around you (solicited or not), your reactions will vary. Sometimes your gut reaction might be, *Nope. Please stop talking.* Sometimes you might think, *Ooooh! Yes, please! Something about this just feels right.* And sometimes you might think, *Hmmm, I'm kind of intrigued, but I need to find out more.*

It's your job to notice how you feel about the opinions flying around you. That's how you figure out if you're getting good advice or if it's just noise. Because what's good for one person might be noise to another, and this is *your* career we're talking about. You don't have to take any advice that doesn't feel right. Remember, *you* are the only expert on you. So the next time someone gives you their two cents, or offers a job hookup you don't want, feel free to nod politely while quietly telling yourself, *Fuck no. Not a chance in hell.*

Notice how you feel about the
opinions flying around you.

5
UH, NEVER MIND

Y ou might feel like we've reeeeeally gone down the rabbit hole. Things are starting to get real. Kinda seems like there's a lot of work involved in this career thing, and maybe you're thinking you should just take some time off. Or travel for a little while. Or go to grad school instead. And maybe you do need that. But you know this career stuff will just be waiting for you when you're done, right?

If you're feeling the urge to chicken out, to give up on the quest for feel-good work, or to bolt from whatever it is you want to do because it just seems too damn hard, you're not alone. A lot of people put off starting their careers, or cave and settle for something less than what they want because all of this career stuff requires not just decision-making (which is hard enough) but also *action*.

Now, you're not the type of person to just cave and settle (if you were, you wouldn't be reading this book), but what you do have are *excuses*. Excuses that you probably think are totally legit. In fact you're probably pissed that I'm calling your tooooootally legit reasons for not moving forward *excuses*. The struggle is real! BTW, no judgment. We all have excuses that get in our way, myself included.

So I'm not going to strip you of your excuses. What I am going to do is help you shine a light on them, so you can see just how bullshit some of them really are. (It's done with love, I promise.)

Some of your excuses might sound like this . . .

- *I have a liberal arts degree. What the hell am I supposed to do with that?*
- *I partied too much in college, and now I have nothing on my resume.*
- *I'm just a chick from a little fishing village. Who the hell do I think I am to make it in the fashion industry?*
- *I don't have any good references. I'm screwed.*
- *But I've never worked in television. My degree is in business.*
- *My grades aren't good enough to get into grad school, so basically, I'm fucked.*
- *I literally have zero contacts in the start-up world. There's no way I'll be able to get my foot in the door.*

And the list goes on . . . and on and on. I don't have

enough education, money, contacts, experience . . . blah, blah, blah.

I'm not trying to be harsh. I'm not. It's just that when you boil them down, all excuses follow the same boring formula:

I can't _____
because _____.

Go ahead and get real about your excuses. Maybe even write 'em down. Especially the ones you're already sensing are kind of bullshit. And hey, listen, don't be ashamed of them. Everybody plays an excuse card now and then — you, me, everybody. But excuses do us more harm than good.

If everybody leaned on their excuses, nothing would ever get done. So we're going to take those excuses of yours and reframe them.

⇒ EXCUSES VS. CONSTRAINTS ⇐

Excuses are what you dish out when you're playing the victim — when you dig in your heels, fold your arms, and throw a pity party for one. We use excuses when we want to shut down the conversation (even if it's only with ourselves), or when we want to feel righteous about not moving forward.

Constraints, on the other hand, are just realities to be dealt with as you move forward — things to take into consideration as you cook up a plan for going after what you want.

What a lot of people do is take a factual, actual constraint (a reality to deal with) and blow it up into an excuse (a bullshit justification for not moving forward). Here's the difference:

CONSTRAINT	EXCUSE
I have a business degree.	I can't work in television because I have a business degree.
I don't have any contacts in the start-up world.	I'll never get my foot in the door at a start-up because I don't have any contacts.
My grades aren't good.	My grades aren't good enough for grad school, so basically, I'm fucked. I'll never get a job or a lover, so I'll have to adopt 12 cats and feed them on food stamps, and I'll die penniless and alone.

Okay, things got a little crazy with that last one, but you get the gist.

When you separate your despair from the facts, you're just left with constraints — limitations you have to work with as you move forward. Facts, not drama. You can suck the drama out of your excuses until you're left with just the facts — legit constraints. That's something you can actually work with.

So maybe you want to go into fashion, but you didn't have access to the spring runways in Bryant Park or pattern drafting from Parsons. Newsflash: Most of the people in fashion didn't either. They used what they had, worked with the constraints they were dealt, and made shit happen. That's how life works, my friend.

Maybe you don't have the contacts or the degree or money or experience you think you need. There are gazillions of ways to break into any career, including making shit up on your own (that's what entrepreneurship is). Your constraints just mean that you arrive at your goal by taking Path B, C, or D instead of Path A. It's all good. Just get creative and get moving.

Suck the drama out of your excuses until you're left with just the facts.

➾ FAULTY PROGRAMMING ⬅

While we're taking an honest look at your excuses, let's also examine your *assumptions* — the stuff you accept as fact and base your decisions upon. Here's a common assumption that a lot of people treat as gospel:

You need a degree in _____
to be a _____.

As in, you need a degree in journalism to become a journalist. (Nope.) As in, you need a business degree to work in business. (Everything is business, dude.) As in, you need an MFA to become an artist. (Um, I don't think Leonardo da Vinci had one.)

For *some* careers, this logic is true (you sure as hell want your doctor to have a medical degree), but for the vast majority of careers, this idea — this thing we blindly accept as fact — is total bullshit. I bet you didn't know that three quarters of college grads work in a field unrelated to their degree. That's *most* people. It's the *norm*.

Same goes for some other career-related "facts" that you may believe. Like this one popular with parents everywhere: *The only way to have a stable career is to lock into a good union job with a pension.* Really? Thirty-five percent of people work for themselves now. And people change jobs an average of

12 times from their mid-20s to their mid-40s. Maybe they know something you don't.

My point is you may be feeding yourself some faulty information.

Whatever beliefs and assumptions you have, they're influencing the decisions you make. Which is why getting really honest about your assumptions — and *checking them* — is a good thing. Because my guess is that they're holding you back.

Fern is a recent grad and a talented writer. She worked three unpaid internships in publishing and editing and built a respectable portfolio. But she lacked confidence. Since her internships were unpaid, she assumed they wouldn't be perceived as relevant experience, and as a result, she talked herself out of applying for the entry-level writing jobs she wanted. That assumption — *my internships won't be perceived as relevant experience* — was holding her back.

> You may be feeding yourself
> some faulty information.

Kyla was already a couple of years into her career, and even though she didn't enjoy her job, she was good at it. But Kyla had an assumption: *I can't be successful at something new.* Let me tell you, it's really freaking hard to even consider moving your career in *any* new direction when you believe that.

Kiara studied international development but secretly

wanted to work in the traditional business world. It was a hard career path to consider pursuing because she held some painful beliefs about "honorable" work. She wondered, *Can I still be a good person if I don't work in international development?*

What are some of your own assumptions? There's only one way to find out if that stuff is true or not: Do your research. Challenge your thinking. But you probably already have a hunch that you're dealing with some faulty information.

⇒ UNINSTALLING THE SOFTWARE ⇐

Some of the faulty information you're carrying around probably isn't even yours. It was given to you by somebody else — like something a teacher taught you to believe, or something a parent did or said to make you see the world in a certain way. We tend to absorb and internalize the beliefs of our parents. Thoughts and beliefs can work like osmosis that way. It just happens, whether it's intentional or not. In fact, it's possible that even your parents didn't intend for you to internalize their beliefs, but we so easily absorb what we're repeatedly exposed to.

Since that happens to all of us, there's an important question you should ask yourself: *Is this belief even mine, or does it belong to someone else?*

Pat is a client of mine who absorbed the belief that "psychology is bullshit" from his dad, and it nearly prevented him from taking his career in that direction. Sheri had a strong interest in design, but her father told her that design wasn't practical, so she became a financial analyst instead. Samantha was raised in a family with a "suck it up and tough it out" mentality. She struggled to leave an abusive employer, framing the decision to leave as a weakness, a personal failure to toughen up and persevere.

Beliefs that were given to you by someone else (often at a young age) are like software that isn't part of the original operating system but was installed by someone else. And if that software is fucking up your operating system, you have to find a way to uninstall it. Otherwise it's just going to keep auto-updating, and you'll wonder why you keep making decisions that don't feel good for you.

Is this belief even mine, or does it belong to someone else?

Whew! You probably need a nap right about now. Getting honest about your excuses and assumptions is heavy. Kudos to you! Now let's talk about the wild party that is . . .

➡ RESISTANCE, AVOIDANCE, AND PROCRASTINATION ⬅

There are two main reasons why people resist, avoid, and procrastinate:

1. They really don't want to do the thing (e.g., do the dishes, write the paper, mow the lawn, etc.).
2. They really DO want to do the thing, but the thought of doing the thing scares the living shit out of them (e.g., applying for that job you really want).

As you try to create a feel-good career, you're definitely likely to run into more of the second variety. Because when you really want something, the stakes feel really high, and the thought of failure is almost paralyzing. If you feel kind of stupefied with some of this career stuff, you know what I'm talking about.

Maybe you think procrastination is just your way of dealing with things — a method to your madness. After all, it worked for you in college, right? You'd wait until the last minute, then get a sudden surge of motivation at the eleventh hour and manage to get everything done on time. You work well under pressure. Procrastination is *your thing*.

Here's why that won't work for you in starting your career: There's no deadline to force you into action. Unless you count death. And that's a long way off (fingers crossed). So let's get honest about your procrastination habits like we did for your assumptions and excuses.

The things we do to procrastinate can be pretty ridiculous. Like sleeping in. Not because you're tired but because you don't want to do that thing you have to do in the morning. Or eating. You're not really hungry, you just need an excuse not to work on that thing. (Or is it just me?) Or scrolling mindlessly on Instagram. After a certain amount of time, it's not even fun anymore, but it sure beats tackling that scary project.

Here are some of the things I do when I'm procrastinating. Fuck, this is embarrassing:

- Do household chores I don't even really give a shit about. Like organizing the silverware drawer.
- Convince myself I need a nap.
- Eat. Eat anything. Carby sweets are a bonus.
- Stare into the open refrigerator.
- See how many likes I got on that post. (Ugh, sad but true.)
- Organize my desktop.
- Make a grocery list.
- Look at my calendar for next week.
- Make a to-do list of the shit I've already done and check off the items (please, god, tell me I'm not the only one who does this).

What kind of things do *you* do to procrastinate? Think about it, and see if any themes emerge. Two main themes emerge from my own list — eating and organizing. If I'm sweeping the cupboards for something carby, I'm probably procrastinating. Same if I'm organizing some unimportant detail. When I notice those red flags, I know I'm avoiding something, and I should probably just bite the bullet (not the donut) and do it.

Now, those things are what I'd call short-term procrastination — quick and convenient little distractions you use to avoid something else you should be doing. But there's also long-term procrastination. Like when you make up some large bullshit project you convince yourself you have to do first before you can actually do the thing that's intimidating you. That's avoidance that you can cleverly blame on your calendar, saying, *Yeah, I'm tooooootally going to get to it, but I'm just really busy with this other thing right now*.

You may find yourself saying things like:

> *Yeah, I'm definitely going to revamp my resume and put myself out there, but my sister needs so much help with her wedding. I'll get to it after all of that's over.*

OR

> *I really want to focus on my health right now, ya know? I'm gonna devote the next few months to getting into better shape. I'll tackle this career stuff after that.*

OR

> *I need to do more research. Once I get through the 10 career and self-help books on my bedside table, we can talk about moving into action. But for now what I need is more information. Speaking of which, maybe there's another class I should take first.*

Each of these scenarios is presented as a seemingly legit diversion of attention, but they're really convenient cop-outs. The convenient cop-out formula goes like this: *I can't do X until I do Y*, where X is the scary but desirable thing that on some level you want to do, and Y is the justifiable distraction you're using to procrastinate from doing it. If there's something you know you want to do, but you never seem to get to it because other stuff gets in the way, it's time you start asking yourself, *Do I really need to do this, or am I just looking for a convenient cop-out?*

> *Do I really need to do this, or am I just looking for a convenient cop-out?*

Now let's talk about one more common form of procrastination. And don't get your panties in a knot . . .

➥ GRAD SCHOOL ⬅

First, let me start by saying that grad school is lovely. I have two master's degrees (I got one while working full time and the other about a decade into my career), and I'm super proud of them both. But . . .

In many ways, grad school is the new gap year. It's a placeholder — the go-to thing people do when they don't feel quite ready to jump into their careers. And there's nothing inherently wrong with that if you have the means to pay for it (or if your parents do), or if a graduate degree is required for your chosen profession (spoiler alert: for most, it's not). The truth is, for many, grad school is an expensive form of procrastination. So if you're thinking about grad school or any other form of additional education, please just take a moment to honestly consider this question: *Do I really need to go back to school?*

If the answer is yes, then more power to you, my friend. Cheers to higher learning!

If the answer is no, but you really *want* to go, and you have the means to do it without getting into a mountain of debt, more power to you, too! But also consider that you're spending not just money but also time (years) and energy. Sometimes it's so totally worth it, and sometimes it's not. Only you know.

> Sometimes it's so totally worth it,
> and sometimes it's not. Only you know.

If the answer is no — there's no actual need to go back to school, and you don't have the cash — then maybe going back to school isn't for you. Not right now, anyway. There are a gazillion paths to most careers, remember? Just choose a different one.

✏️ GIVING UP AT 90% ✏️

I have a crush. Literally right this second as I'm writing this, I'm crushing on someone. I have been for a couple of months. Allow me to pause here for a second to share that I am *not* the kind of person who makes the first move. I hardly even flirt. I live way at the other end of the spectrum. If I like somebody, I'm more likely to err on the side of aloof, lest I show my cards and make a fool of myself.

But, like I said, I have a crush. And after about two months of crushing silently, I finally found the nerve to introduce myself to him. Yes, it took two months of dry-mouth jitters just to say hello. (A part of me will always be a shy kid at a middle school dance, shuffling her feet, back against the gymnasium wall.)

My crush works in the same office building as me, just down the hall from my own office. Now that we've met, he pops in every day to say hello and have a little chat. We're both at work, so we keep it profesh, but there's a spark, and the more I get to know him, the more I like him. This has been going on for about two weeks now. It's delicious, and it's also KILLING ME. He's never mentioned a wife or girl-friend, but I'm desperate to know if this is going anywhere. *Does this guy who gives me the flutters like me? Is he even single?*

So after two weeks of wondering and hoping and flutters, I got brave. I just asked. I took a deep breath, and it felt like an eternity for me to finally meet his eyes with my own when I said, "I like you. Are you seeing anybody?"

Why am I sharing this story with you?

This isn't just about my handsome mancrush down the hall. Not really. This is about *desire*. And more specifically, this is about *showing up* for your desire. It's about taking a risk and saying *I want this* without knowing how things will turn out. This is about having skin in the game — not just in love but in life, in your career.

If feels safer to keep your desire hidden — to lock it up and insulate it from the elements, to shelter it from judgment and rejection. And the truth is it *is* safer. If you put your desire on lockdown, and if you never put yourself out there, you can't get hurt. On the other hand, you also can't get what you want. That's a shitty trade-off if you ask me.

To get what you want, you have to step out from behind the security of feigned ambivalence. You have to admit what you want and ask for it. You have to make the first move. There's no getting around this in the world of work. Your dream job can't swipe right or meet you at a bar. You have to initiate. Otherwise you'll stay stuck in career purgatory, waiting waiting waiting, but never moving forward.

A lot of people are really good at *starting* to move forward in their career or, in many cases, *pretending* to move forward. They identify a general direction they want to go in and then take a half-assed crack at it. They'll apply for a couple of jobs but submit them with a shitty resume or a generic, vanilla cover letter. Or they'll start a project but abandon it when it gets tough. I call this *giving up at 90%* — bailing at a critical moment when success or failure is imminent, after a ton of work has already been put in and a final push is all that's required.

A friend of mine is a professionally trained actor. For years after he graduated, he would book auditions but then not show up. He busted his ass in school for years, poured blood, sweat, and tears into his training (not to mention tons of time and money), found auditions, booked the auditions, and then bailed by refusing to show up. It's been years since then, and thankfully he found his way back to acting, but he knows exactly what he was up to back then. "I knew there was a decent chance I'd get rejected," he said. "It felt safer not to try. Because that way, you can't fail."

Your dream job can't swipe right or meet you at a bar. You have to initiate.

That's what I mean by giving up at 90%. It's that *fuck it* mentality when you panic or rage-quit close to the finish line because you're afraid to fail, saying, *You know what? I'm OUT. Peace.* Or when you lie to yourself, saying, *I don't really care about this after all*, when really, you're just chickenshit.

We do this not out of ambivalence or detachment but out of fear. When you really want something, going for it makes you feel vulnerable and tender and exposed. You think, *What if I try and they laugh at me? Or what if they say I'm no good?*

What if people think this is stupid? What if I'm ignored? Or what if I get what I want, but I fuck it up and fall flat on my face?

It's tempting to push down your desire. Because the stakes just feel too high. (And nobody can laugh at your desire or dismiss it if they can't see it, right?) But when you ghost your desire — when you abandon it just as you're getting to know it — you never find out what might have been. That's why you have to let your desires be known and why you have to go for it. Because *what if?*

The question *what if* goes both ways. What if you go for what you want, and you don't get it? That'll hurt. You'll feel disappointed. Then again, the sting of disappointment is less painful than the lingering ache of regret. Because what if you open up your soft, squishy heart and find the guts to say, *I want this*, and then what if you actually *get* it? Might be worth the risk, right?

The sting of
disappointment is
less painful than
the lingering ache
of regret.

6

BUT I DON'T KNOW
WHAT I'M DOING

You probably feel like you're supposed to know what your dream job is and how to get it — that you're supposed to have a clear vision for your future and a solid plan to pay off all of that student debt. You're supposed to know how to make your parents proud and make a whack of cash, kicking ass and taking numbers along the way, right?

Oh, honey, no.

You're not supposed to know how to do any of that. And I'm going to let you in on some classified information: Nobody really knows. None of us out here knows what the fuck we're doing. It's one of the secrets of adulthood. We've all just quietly agreed to not talk about it and to pretend that everything is fine.

I'll probably get in trouble for sharing this classified info.

Because we're not supposed to tell the rookies. That's against the rules. Whenever someone steps out of line and lets the cat out of the bag, everyone is like, *Shhhhh! JUST BE COOL.* And then that person gets bound and gagged and dragged off to a room with no windows and no Wi-Fi.

You've probably spent your entire life surrounded by adults doing the *JUST BE COOL* poker face thing — your teachers, your colleagues, and *definitely* your parents. The first rule in the parenting playbook is *JUST BE COOL and pretend you've got it all under control.* Go ahead and ask your mom. She'll probably be relieved that she can finally give up the façade after more than two decades of faking it.

> ## None of us out here knows what the fuck we're doing.

Adults pretend to have the answers because they don't want you to get scared, but the truth is, it's a goddamn crapshoot out here. So if you feel like you don't know what you're doing, that's just totally normal. Nobody really does. And you can consider this newfound knowledge that none of us knows what we're doing a rite of passage into adulthood. You're one of us now.

Here's the good news: You don't have to know what you're doing or have it all figured out in order to make a plan. And, yes, we have come to the point where you're ready to make a plan . . . even if you feel like you're *not* ready.

Because nobody would ever do anything if they waited until they felt ready.

⟹ A LOOSE PLAN ⟸

We're going to create a plan. A *loose* plan. One that is flexible and adaptable and can change as you change. Fill your plan with too much detail, and you'll feel overwhelmed and paralyzed. And you know what? Paralyzed isn't exactly an ideal state of being. If you've ever felt totally stuck, you know what I mean. A *loose* plan is where it's at.

Think of your career as a road trip — full of adventure and surprises, with lots of stops along the way. You know who never gets invited on road trips? Carol. Carol is that control freak you used to be friends with and went on a road trip with once. Carol was always reminding you of the schedule, looking at her watch, tapping her foot, and checking the map. Her obsessive list-making and time-checking made you want to "accidentally" leave her stranded by a roadside truck stop. Chick couldn't go with the flow. And road trips are no fun unless you go with the flow. Sure, you can make a plan, but you also have to chill out a little and follow adventure. It's like that with your career, too.

Sure, you can make a plan, but you also have to chill out a little and follow adventure.

There are two ways you can create a loose career plan. One way is to plan ahead and reverse engineer, to keep your eye on the prize (that thing you want to do for your career) and then break down the path to get there into manageable steps. This is an awesome strategy if you know what you want to do for your career. If you *don't* know what you want to do for your career, the other way of creating a loose career plan is to feel it out and just take things one step at a time. We'll get to that second strategy in a minute, but first let's talk about . . .

➥ REVERSE ENGINEERING ⬅

If you know what you want, that's amazing. Seriously, it's half the battle. But knowing what you want can also be stressful if you don't have a plan to get it. Which is where reverse engineering comes in.

If you know what you want for your career, imagine that thing as a set of precise GPS coordinates. (Actually, even if you *don't* know exactly what you want, you can still play along — just imagine one of the things you think you *might* want.) When you want to get to a place you've never been to before, what's the first thing you do? If you're anything like me, you pop it into your Google Maps app, and BINGO, you can see the route to get there. You can see several routes, actually. And you can choose which route to take. You can choose the fastest route, or the scenic route, or the most familiar route. It's up to you.

Since Google hasn't invented a handy little career navigation app yet (maybe it's just a matter of time?), we have to plan out a route ourselves. Which is no problem, actually. You've already been gathering the information you need — by narrowing down what you want, doing your research, and talking to people in those fields. Remember your informational interviews? Those conversations have given you a massive amount of information. Now you're going to use it.

From the research you've done and the people you talked to, you actually know a lot about the various things people have done to get to your preferred (or potential) career destination. And you've likely noticed that none of the people you spoke to took exactly the same path. Go back to your notes from your informational interviews and read what people said about how they got where they are.

For example, let's say you spoke to a bunch of people working in event management because that's what you want to do. Your list might look something like this:

Things people did to get a career in event management:

- Sat on the charity events board for the local hospital
- Completed a hospitality degree
- Got an event management certificate
- Joined a national event management association and attended conferences

- Got an entry-level job working for a hotel's corporate conference division
- Worked a weekend job assisting a wedding planner
- Completed an internship running events for local historical society
- Got a job working as a junior project manager
- Started their own event management company on the side
- Volunteered for the documentary film festival

Now I'm going to ask you to be a little bit cutthroat. If any of the things that people have done to get to where you want to go seem totally unappealing to you, cross it off the list. For example, if you know getting another degree would feel like a two-year drive through Jurassic Park in a hamster ball, strike it as an option. If dealing with emotional brides would drive you crazy, that's gotta go, too. Or if the thought of running your own business would feel like one giant cake wreck, it's not for you. Whittle down your list of possible paths. Because, remember: there are many routes to your destination and we only want you to choose one that feels good to you.

Are there some things remaining on your list that seem kind of interesting but don't quite hit the mark? You can tweak a couple of those items. For example, let's say hospitals give you the willies, but you'd totally love to sit on the events board for another kind of charity — maybe Big Brothers or something. And while you're open to an internship, the local historical society seems like a snoozefest. Helping with events for an art gallery would be way more interesting to you. And you're not really into documentaries, but you'd totally volunteer for a theatre festival. Tweak some of the items on your list to make it more interesting, more *you*. You can also feel free to add things to the list. You probably have some ideas of your own for getting where you want to go. This is *your* career we're talking about. Make it your own.

What you'll have when you've done that are some mighty fine options for moving in the right direction. That's what a loose plan looks like. There's no reason why you can't start to tackle some of the stuff at the top of that list right now. Like, today. Get moving.

Even if you know what you want, and even if you have the "right" degree, and even if you have a solid plan, this phase is scary AF. Because you've never done it before. And, let's be honest, there's a big difference between *learning* about something and *doing* it. That's why moving into your career is so freaking hard — you feel like a fraudulent imposter half of the time because everything is so goddamn new. One of my clients panicked about her transition from law school to her career. She said, "Technically I know this stuff, but I've never actually *practiced* law before." So she reverse engineered it by networking her ass off, talking to lots of other lawyers, and cooking up a little plan. Even though it scared the crap out of her.

Another client of mine was a mortgage underwriter who wanted to climb the corporate ladder fast. She reverse engineered that by talking to more senior underwriters and even joining a formal mentorship program, and then taking the advice she received and running with it. Two of my clients wanted to start their own private counseling practice. So they talked to other counselors, learned more about the ups and downs of running your own practice, and then slowly built a website and a brand and a couple of offerings, and *voilà*, suddenly they had a private practice. Another client started her career in IT sales but wanted to pivot to compliance and risk management, so she talked to people in that field, revamped her resume, rebranded herself on LinkedIn, and applied for jobs that were related to her new focus. She scored three interviews in the span of a week. Sometimes it can be that easy. You just have to make a little plan and get going. And are you noticing the pattern here? Figure out what you want, talk to people doing that, borrow and adapt the bits that sound good to you, make your plan, and then actually *do* it.

But a word to the wise: Plan out your path in pencil, not permanent marker. And, for heaven's sake, definitely not embossed gold leaf. What I mean is: Don't clutch your plan too tightly, even if you know what you want and you're reverse engineering. When your plan is too detailed or too rigid, you suffocate any potential for spontaneity. Even the best plans need to be adaptable. Because life happens. At some point you will redraw some of the lines on your map. So proceed toward what you want with passion, but keep that pencil tucked behind your ear.

Plan out your path in pencil, not permanent marker.

➡ FEELING IT OUT ⬅

If reverse engineering is like plugging your career destination into Google Maps, then feeling it out is like working with an old-school compass — the kind you hope you have when you're lost in the woods. Feeling it out is an awesome way to build a loose career plan if there are a couple of things you're interested in, but you're not really sure which way to go.

Make a mental list of two or three of the things you're considering doing with your career. Now, even though you may feel uncertain about which path is right for you, you've also talked to people working in each of those areas. (Right?! Informational interviews!) Recall the many different things the people you talked to did to get to those jobs — the steps they took to get where they are.

Of the information you gathered about the many paths to get there, what routes would you consider taking? What routes would you definitely *not* consider taking? Don't do any of the shit that doesn't appeal to you. And remember you can get creative here, too. There are almost certainly some unconventional routes that the people you spoke to didn't even mention (or consider themselves). What might be fun to try? And how could you make it your own?

You can't do everything at once anyway, so why not start by trying the things that pique your interest the most. That's how you feel things out — by sensing the next move one baby step at a time, not by building a master plan. Because let's be honest, people who build master plans often end up changing them drastically, anyway . . . because first of all, there's always new information to work with, and second, people are constantly evolving and changing, so what they want also evolves and changes.

One of my clients, Rachel, is a corporate trainer who is curious about possibly becoming a UX designer. So she's exploring it first by just taking a single course in UX design. Same for Monique, who is an executive assistant who wants to move into communications. She's starting with a class to see how she likes it.

Marty is a finance hotshot who wants to create his own investment product and bring it to market. He's half planning it, half winging it — bringing the right team together, providing leadership, and adapting as he goes.

Denise is starting a coaching and training company, but felt really stuck between two ideas for the type of service she wanted to offer and the type of people she wanted to serve. Instead of deliberating forever, she took a couple of weeks to think it over and then thought, *Geez, this could go on forever. Fuck it, I'll try THIS one.* She got moving. She knows she can always pivot and rebrand if she needs to.

Gillian is writing a book. There are 101 ways she could have begun, but instead of evaluating them all, she just got started. Even though she felt like she didn't know what the hell she was doing. Because she knows she could have thought about it forever instead of actually writing.

Let's be honest, people who build master plans often end up changing them drastically, anyway.

You don't have to have the whole thing mapped out in exacting detail before you start. Sometimes it's better to just try it on and see how it goes. You may find you actually waste a lot less time that way. There are so many people who stay stuck in planning/thinking mode (instead of *doing* mode) for years.

Start moving forward by trying a couple of things that feel exciting to you. You can certainly try some other things later, but why not start with the things that feel the best right now. As you get moving, you'll get more information. Stuff like:

- *Jesus Christ, what is this, the Hunger Games?! Hard pass.*
- *Wow, I'm really good at this! Somebody call Hollywood and tell them I'm ready for my sassy career woman biopic!*
- *My boss is a raging sociopath, and my coworkers are human Muppets. DO NOT WANT.*
- *Wheee! I feel just like Elle Woods when she kicked Warner's ass at Harvard. This is fun!*
- *Hello, police? I'd like to turn myself in. Living in prison would literally be better than this.*
- *I had no idea work could be this good! It's like I'm at Hogwarts, and the sorting hat created a special house just for me!*

Consider information like this your compass's way of trying to point you due north. Pay attention to the signs along the way, make a change when necessary, and you'll end up somewhere awesome.

⟹ SHOULD I REVERSE ENGINEER OR FEEL IT OUT? ⟸

When I was 23, with a bright, shiny Bachelor of Journalism in my hand, I felt totally lost. My time at journalism school basically confirmed that being a journalist wasn't for me. I

You don't have to
have the whole thing
mapped out in exacting
detail before you start.

didn't like it that much. Oh sure, I *could* have worked as a journalist, but the signs said no, and so I listened to the signs.

But what to do in the meantime, right? I had a mountain of student debt, so I did one of the smartest things I could have done in my situation (though it wasn't glamorous) — I worked a shit retail job for a couple of months while I figured things out.

Eventually I scored a gig working as a recruiter at my old university. It was something I just tried on a whim, and I discovered I LOVED it. For the next six years, I held a handful of pretty awesome jobs for that department and worked my way up with promotions and better pay. I also did my first master's degree during evenings and weekends, which — ka-ching! — my employer helped to pay for.

I loved my master's degree so much, I thought I'd get a PhD and become a professor. So I left my stable gig and went back to school full time. This did not work out so well. I loved teaching, but I hated conducting research. I was getting that nagging feeling that I was in the wrong place (which, like most people, I ignored for a couple of years). To keep myself sane in a job I hated I got some coach training. I wasn't sure what I'd do with it, but it just felt right.

My new plan was to finish my PhD and then quit my teaching job and start a coaching practice. It seemed like a good plan on paper except for one small detail: I haaaaated conducting research for my PhD. And teaching as a professor wasn't enough to make up for that.

So I quit. Four years and 93 pages into my dissertation.

Hardest decision I've ever made. Also the best. I kept my teaching gig for four months while I built my coaching practice, and here we are a few years later.

Which strategy did I use to build my career path? Did I reverse engineer or feel it out? Both, actually. I reverse engineered as I moved up in my recruiting gig. And also as I planned my coaching business. I saw things I wanted, and I made a plan to go after them — promotions, a master's degree, coach training, and building a business. But I had to feel it out when I was lost after graduation, and also when I realized I was in a job I hated and didn't know what to do next. All I could do then was give myself the time and space to feel things out. So I kept the less-than-ideal job for a while and secretly plotted my escape.

Navigating your career will be like that, too — a dance between reverse engineering and feeling it out. That's how it is for everyone, whether they realize it or not. And sometimes you'll reverse engineer your way to a path that feels good for a little while . . . until suddenly it doesn't anymore. That's when it's time to switch to feeling it out again.

Renata started her career in the music production and distribution business — an enviable gig that looks super sexy on paper, and that many people would be psyched to have. But after a while, she found that there was nowhere to grow — at least not in the ways she wanted to. She has a Bachelor of Commerce and considered working in areas like tech, design, communications, advertising, and project management. The fact that her interests were wide and varied stressed her out. Would she ever be able to pick something?! Whatever area she decided to work in, Renata knew that it had to be creative, collaborative, innovative, interdisciplinary, project-based, and not super corporate. She thought her skills and experience and interests aligned perfectly for project management. She wanted to give it a try. But would she be able to find a hip, chill company to work for? She did. Renata became a project manager at a cool, non-corporate design consulting firm — giving her not only fulfilling work she can sink her teeth into, but also the kind of work culture she wanted. Yes please!

Ivy started her career in marketing but wanted to switch gears and become a real estate agent. She learned more about it by talking to other agents. She liked what she learned, got certified, and is now a realtor.

Jessie started a career in television, but found he wasn't making as much progress as he wanted. After a few frustrating years of shitty-paying freelance work, he was like, *Fuck this noise*, and slowly made his way to a career in advertising.

All of these people started on one path and at some point felt compelled to make a change. That will probably happen to you at some point in your career, too. When it does, you'll be ready for it — reverse engineering when you have a destination in mind, and feeling it out when the details seem fuzzy.

⇛ PARALLEL TRACKS ⇚

Some careers are tougher to break into, and that's just the truth.

Maybe you want to be in musical theatre, or to be an Instagram influencer, or a fashion blogger, or a food critic, or an aerial yoga instructor, or a stage combat fight director. Some gigs really make you work for it before it pays off. You have to bust your ass and hustle for it first. Sometimes for years.

That's no reason to give up on your vision of becoming an aerial yoga instructor. (I mean, *somebody's* getting paid to do that supercool shit, so it might as well be you.) But also, you may have to be a little patient with it, a little stealthier in your approach. It may take some time. And, luckily, you've got time.

Most people aren't too creative when it comes to how they think about their career. They think, *You pick a thing. You do the thing. End of story.* It's a pretty old-school way of thinking. But more and more, people are getting waaaaay more creative about how they think about their careers, and they're choosing *parallel tracks* . . . which is the career equivalent of having your cake and being able to pay for it, too.

Let's say you want to pursue a career that's tough to break

into, or is super intermittent, or pays peanuts (or nothing at all). If it's something that matters to you, I really think you ought to stick with it. But also, a person's gotta eat. And pay rent. And chip away at those student debt installments.

There's actually no reason why you can't do all of those things. Spend some of your time and energy on the thing you're super passionate about (even if it doesn't bring home the bacon), and spend some of your time and energy on something else you like that *does* bring home the bacon. Track 1 fills you up emotionally, and Track 2 fills you up literally. With bacon.

Track 2 can be the very thing that makes Track 1 possible. For example:

- Working a serving gig so you can have the flexibility to perform in musical theatre. I have a friend who does that.
- Working as a consultant by day and writing your novel by night. A colleague of mine does that.
- Working for a start-up and also producing your own indie theatre shows. A friend of mine does that.
- Working as a lawyer while you grow your photography business until the point that you can quit your job as a law associate. The woman who took the photo at the back of this book did that.
- Working as a professor while you get your business off the ground. I did that.

I could keep going, but you get the point. If the thing you want to do isn't going to pay the bills (at least not right away), don't give up on it. Just add another track. And make sure it's something else you enjoy. (Maybe you don't love it as much as the thing you've got going on in Track 1, but make it something you like.) Juggling two tracks can be tricky, but it's almost always worth it if it keeps something you love in your life.

Parallel tracks: the career equivalent of having your cake and being able to pay for it, too.

Think of your career as the scaffolding surrounding the life you're trying to build. Use it to support the things you want to do.

7

STUDENT DEBT: A SAD TROMBONE

Maybe you're getting sick of holding your breath and crossing your fingers every time you splurge for guac.

Maybe you're *this* close to signing up as a sugar baby on SeekingArrangement. (Ew.)

Maybe you're thinking, *Jeez, if Kanye can't make it financially, what hope is there for the rest of us?*

I mean, you're all for figuring out what you want in your career, and we're totally working on that, but in the meantime you need to GET. PAID. Like, as soon as possible.

Do you have student debt? Most people do. There's no shame in that. But it sure is stressful.

If you're anything like I was when I was in your shoes, that student debt feels like a monkey on your back — a sweaty, annoying, constant reminder of what you owe. And you probably want to get that hairy little beast off your back as soon as possible.

My parents couldn't afford to put me through school, so I paid for my degree myself by cobbling together a bunch of part-time jobs and student loans. I was grateful for the chance to go to school, but I *hated* the heavy feeling of being in debt, so I got really serious about paying it off as quickly as possible.

Even when I was working a shit retail job living in an expensive city, I saved money to pay off my debt. I lived in a crappy apartment with three other girls, upstairs from a bunch of douchey frat boys, behind a fish market in Chinatown. It was smelly. (There was a garbage worker's strike that summer. Yuck.) It was noisy. (Aforementioned frat boys.) It was small. It was also JUST FINE. It wasn't glamorous, but I had everything I needed. Plus, I didn't exactly expect to be living a Kardashian life right after graduation.

I was figuring things out and slowly paying off my debt. Four months later, when I got my first real grown-up job that paid real grown-up dollars, I paid off even more. So if you're in debt, I feel you. And I want you to know it doesn't have to paralyze you.

The great thing about being out of school and starting your career is that you're about to start the part of your life where you actually make money. Decent money. Many of those grown-up dollars will help you pay off that student debt, and before you know it you'll bring that number down to a big, fat zero. At which point you'll celebrate like crazy (in an understated, fiscally responsible way).

Do you have a budget yet? You should. Because you need to track where your dollars are coming from and where they're going. Even if you think you don't need a budget, you do. Budgets can be verrrrry eye opening. A client of mine was super stressed about cash, so I told her to make a budget and track her expenses. She did, and she realized she was spending more than half of her grown-up paycheck on takeout and booze. MORE THAN HALF. Make a budget. Notice where you're spending. Adjust accordingly.

Maybe you'll notice you need to haul your ass to the less expensive grocery store. Or cut back on your Uber allowance. Or on your Sephora spending. Or on that $12 cold-pressed juice you buy every single day. I'm just saying.

It's tempting to just say *fuck it* when you're already in debt. Especially with little purchases here and there. I mean, what's $50 when you're already one billion dollars in debt, right? Especially when you've had a shit day and are stressed out and really *deserve* that new sweater or those after-work drinks or that really sick tattoo you've been meaning to get forever anyway. But things like sweaters and drinks, and even ink, add up in a hurry. If you're not paying attention, you'll think your bank account has been hacked when really you just pissed away your money all by yourself.

I made my first budget as soon as I finished undergrad. I knew I'd have to start making student debt payments soon, and I needed a plan. So I made myself a simple little Excel spreadsheet, tracking my income and expenses month by month. I paid off my student debt years ago, but I still keep a budget.

And it's still just an Excel spreadsheet. It's not sexy, but it helps me track and plan just like the grown-ass adult I am.

It's tempting to just say *fuck it* when you're already in debt.

Takeaway: Get yourself a budget. Pronto. Whether it's in a nerdy little Excel spreadsheet or a simple app, just make one. It'll help you chip away at that debt bit by bit just like I did. (BTW, I know budgets seem lame and obvious, but don't knock it until you actually *try* it, okay?) Getting real about your financial situation might *feel* like a restriction, but what you're really doing is choosing something better — freedom. Paying off your debt is temporary. It won't last forever. Keep at it, and you'll get that monkey off your back in no time.

⟱ GOOD INVESTMENT / BAD INVESTMENT ⟰

Now that you're going to budget your dollars like a champ, let's consider the *other* kind of budgets.

Oh, you thought budgeting was just for money? How wrong you are, my friend! There are other things you can budget like a total boss, and I can almost guarantee that you have more of them than you have money. I'm talking about *time* and *energy*.

Huh?

You heard me. Time and energy. You should spend your time and energy like you spend your dollars. Wisely. With intention.

I'm guessing you don't have kids yet. Or maybe you don't even want kids. (If so, ka-ching! You've just saved yourself lots of time, energy, AND money.) If you're out of school, and you're just starting your career, and you don't have kids, you actually have more time and energy at your disposal than most other people on the planet.

Think about where you're spending your free time and energy. What do you do during evenings? What about weekends? If you're not working right now, how do you spend your day? Maybe it's Netflix, the gym, sleeping, reading, Instagram, Tinder, drinks with friends, partying, applying for jobs, shopping, or any number of other things. Make a mental list.

> Spend your time and energy like you spend your dollars. Wisely. With intention.

Got your mental list? Good. Now think about each individual item on your list and decide if it's generally a good investment of your time and energy or if it's generally a bad investment of your time and energy. For example, if the amount of time you spend on Netflix and social media has you feeling like an epic loser, those things are probably a poor investment of your time and energy — which isn't to say you have to go cold turkey; just ease up on that shit. If you feel good about your time at the gym and reading and applying for jobs, then those things are probably good investments of your time and energy.

I will go ahead and admit that I probably spend too much time on social media. Instagram, specifically. It's just so easy. Especially if I just have 10 or 15 minutes to kill between other things. I'll just kind of zone out and start scrolling. And I never really feel like that's a particularly good or rewarding use of my time. So bit by bit, I've started to curb it. I'll throw my phone in a drawer if I want to focus. And I've started keeping books on a side table in my living room, so they're easy to access. That way I can dip into them just as quickly as I can dip into my phone. Plus, reading is actually something I really enjoy, so doing more of it feels like a better investment of my time.

It should go without saying (but I'll say it anyway) that you should spend less time and energy on things that feel like poor investments, and more time and energy on things that feel like good investments. Especially if you're feeling lost or frustrated about your career situation. Sure, have a life, see your friends, binge-watch the new season of *Stranger Things* — but use some of your time and energy to do stuff that will help you get unstuck and move forward. You may not have a ton of cash right now, but you *do* have time and energy. Spend it wisely.

➥ THE OTHER KIND OF STUDENT DEBT ⬅

If you breezed through the first part of this chapter without a care in the world because your parents paid for school and you don't have any student debt, congratulations! (For real. You are the envy of your peers.) Financial debt is a heavy burden to carry. Of course, so is the *other* kind of debt.

The other kind of student debt is not repaid in dollars, but rather in gratitude and obligation.

Maybe your mom found a way to put you through school on her single mother salary. And you're so grateful that you find yourself following her advice . . . even when it's not quite right for you.

Or maybe your parents emigrated from a turbulent country so you could have a chance at a better life. You're the first person in your whole family to go to college . . . and now the burden of that privilege weighs heavily on your career decisions.

Or maybe your parents paid for private school and an Ivy League degree and scored you a prestigious internship . . . and now you feel obligated to do what *they* want you to do for your career instead of what you want.

Financial debt is a heavy burden to carry.
Of course, so is the *other* kind of debt.

That's the other kind of debt — a debt of gratitude and obligation. These kinds of debts can feel just as heavy as financial debts, sometimes even heavier. Because, honestly, how can you ever repay someone for working three jobs just so you could go to school? Or for putting down an insane chunk of cash so you could get the best damn education money can buy? Or for leaving a poverty-stricken or war-torn country just so you could have a better life? Not possible.

These kinds of debts are self-imposed. The terms of repayment aren't set out in black and white like with financial debt. You're not forced to feel gratitude. You're not forced to feel obligation. You just do. And what's tricky is you're never really sure when, if ever, the debt is repaid.

Nine times out of ten, the people who've done things to help you (it's almost always your parents) don't want you living a life of obligation, indebted to them. They usually just want you to be safe and happy, and they may or may not think that involves following their (biased) advice. Remember, only *you* are the expert on you. And grateful or not, this life is yours to live.

Only *you* are the
expert on you.

➡ BUT WHAT IF I LIVE IN MY MOM'S BASEMENT? ⬅

Part of this whole adulting thing means living it up sans financial help from parents. At least that's what you aspire to. But sometimes you're down and out, and if a parent offers you help — like a roof over your head and food to eat — it feels like a godsend.

Well . . . mostly.

It's not that you're not grateful. You so totally *are*, it's just that accepting help from your parents sometimes feels like a failure, or like it comes with strings attached. Oh, nothing crazy, but maybe there's a lecture you have to listen to on a regular basis, or paranoid questions you have to answer, or "friendly advice" you're expected to follow, all because you're getting a handout. And you're super thankful for the help, but, weirdly, it also feels kinda shitty.

So let's talk about making the best of a weird situation. Let's talk about how to be a legit grown-up even if you're living with your parents. This basically boils down to two things: showing appreciation, and not being a dick.

Most people see their parents as one of four things: heroes, total pains in the ass, servants, or human ATMs. At some point in their 20s, people start to realize that their parents are none of these things. Your parents are regular people with shit to do and interests of their own.

That means you should do them the courtesy of not

being a dick, and maybe even show some appreciation. If you haven't done much of that yet, you're not alone. Everyone is a dick to their parents sometimes. Especially during those teenage years. (I know I was.) But there comes a time when things have to change. Like, for example, when your grown ass is living in your mother's basement.

How about politely letting your mom or dad know when you're going to have a late night? Worrying about their offspring is basically coded into their DNA, so cut them a break and be as considerate as you can.

How about doing your own laundry? I mean, you did your own laundry when you were away at school. It's not like you *forgot* how to do laundry.

How about *not* buying the next round of drinks when you're out with your friends and instead using that money to grab some groceries? Pick up your mom's favorite yogurt, and it'll make her head spin.

There are lots of ways you can show appreciation and not be a dick while you're living under your parents' roof. Think of one or two and try them out. Even if you live on your own, it wouldn't kill you to be nicer to your parents.

Another way you can show appreciation and not be a dick is by having an open conversation with your mom or dad about your career and financial situation. Keep them in the loop about how things are going. Because neither you nor they want you living in their basement forever, and one way to keep them from prying is to be transparent.

A client of mine — I'll call him Kamal — was still living

at home with his parents while he figured out his career situation. And things were *tense*. He and his mom kept dancing around the topic of career. She would casually ask how the job hunt was going, and he would feel like a loser and be short-tempered and vague. He would tense up every time she even walked past his room. (I bet she did, too.) She never intended to add extra pressure, and he never intended to snap at her, but that's how it went. Things were actually *worse* because they never had a real conversation about it.

Sometimes the best thing to do is to have the uncomfortable conversation.

Sometimes the best thing to do is to have the uncomfortable conversation. So consider having a grown-up conversation about your exit plan. If you're living at home, tell your mom or dad what you're working on (e.g., reading this book, applying for jobs, etc.) and what kind of timeline you're working with. Things may change, but at least they'll know you're making a serious effort. How the hell are they supposed to know if you don't tell them?

Speaking of making a serious effort to get you out of the basement, sometimes that requires a . . .

⮕ JUST FOR NOW JOB ⬅

Getting a *just for now* job — even if it's not exactly what you want, or even if you haven't figured out what you want yet — can be a really good thing. And yes, a just for now job is exactly what it sounds like. A job. Just for now. A job that will make you some cash while you figure out what you want in the long term. Nobody lands their dream job straight outta school. (Okay, maybe one lucky asshole out of a zillion does.) You might as well make some money and get some experience while you're putting together your master plan.

What kind of jobs would you consider taking just for now while you figure things out? Maybe it's a serving job. Or your job from last summer. Or a not-so-glamorous entry-level job somewhere. Yes, you have a degree now. One you likely paid a fuck-ton of money for. And, yes, you might feel like some jobs are beneath you. But you have to start somewhere. Because your career fairy godmother isn't just going to tap you on the shoulder while you're watching *Broad City* in your unwashed, Dorito-crusted pajamas.

As I mentioned, I graduated with a journalism degree and had no desire to work in journalism. I didn't have a Plan B, and figuring out your career isn't exactly something you can do in a hot second. I knew I needed time to figure things out, but in the meantime, I had to pay rent, buy food, and make student loan installments. So I worked full-time hours at the crappy retail job I had been working at while I was a student. Did I love that job? No. Was I happy to have it? HELL YES. It was a just for now job that let me pay the bills while I figured shit out. I worked it for about four months until I got a legit grown-up job. That next job was just a four-month contract working as a recruiter (something I never expected to do), but I loved it, and it eventually turned into something bigger. I tried it because I needed to pay the bills, and I thought it might seem interesting, and it helped me move in the right direction.

> Your career fairy godmother isn't just going to tap you on the shoulder while you're watching *Broad City* in your unwashed, Dorito-crusted pajamas.

I have a client who is working a couple of food delivery shifts a week while he works on his art. And another who is doing admin work for a couple of months while she waits for her master's degree program to begin. Another took a copywriting contract gig while she weighs her long-term options. One person is keeping her job as a server while she moves into TV production part time. And another is working at a gym while she builds her health coaching business.

So go ahead and apply for a less-than-ideal, just for now job if you think you need more time to figure things out. *Especially* if you need money right away. A just for now job might be exactly what you need to lower your anxiety and pay some bills. Stop waiting and get busy. And more importantly, get *paid*.

But remember that your just for now job is meant to be *just for now*. Forget that, and you're likely to find yourself quietly sobbing in the employee bathroom, feeling hopeless about settling for something less. That's not what you're doing. You're being a responsible grown-up while you figure some shit out and get your game plan together. Keep your eye on the prize, and you'll be just fine.

8
CAREER LEGIT

ake a deep breath. Because we're about to get serious about getting you hired. For a job you actually want. In a field you actually want to be a part of.

If thinking about that makes you roll your eyes or puke in your mouth a little bit, it's very possible that you're dealing with imposter syndrome, which I know sounds like a bullshit, made-up term but is actually a real, scientifically validated thing.

Almost everyone feels a bit of imposter syndrome at the beginning of their career (unless they're an egomaniac or sociopath). Imposter syndrome is that feeling you get when you think the people around you are smarter or more legit than you are — when you think everyone around you is totally out of your league, like you snuck into the VIP lounge, and you just know someone is going to spot you and kick your ass out.

True, you're a career rookie. And true, most of the people you'll be working with have more experience and have been at this thing for longer than you have. But that doesn't mean you don't belong.

➼ BUT I DON'T HAVE ANY EXPERIENCE ⇇

Wrong.

You don't have *as much* experience as many other people, but you *do* have experience. You and your (understandably limited) experience are in exactly the same position as anyone else who ever started their career. All of those people got hired, and you will, too. You just have to start thinking more broadly about what counts as experience. You have to get creative.

Getting creative about your experience does NOT mean making shit up. Don't ever do that. An interviewer will know if you're blowing smoke up their ass. If you're lying, you'll not only feel like an imposter, you'll actually *be* one. Gross.

Getting creative and thinking more broadly about what counts as experience just means thinking outside the box when it comes to identifying and talking about your transferable skills. Yes, we are going to talk about transferable skills. You have more of them than you think you do.

You and your
(understandably limited)
experience are in exactly
the same position as
anyone else who ever
started their career.

Let's take that part-time retail gig, for example. Your boss trusted you enough to close up shop some evenings and do the cash, debit, and credit balances on your own and make bank deposits. Transferable skills! This shows that you're good with numbers and logic, and that you're trustworthy.

And that tree planting you did last summer? How on earth is that relevant to the office job you're applying for? Well, you learned how to get efficient really quickly, so you could maximize your pay. Plus, you were in the top 10% of planters. You're smart, efficient, and know how to hustle.

What about that charity golf tournament you helped organize? Sure, it was volunteer work, but you learned a shit-ton about budgeting, organizing, planning, and managing big-ticket events.

And how about some of your extracurriculars, like organizing film club or coaching little league? Well, you were able to score some awesome venues and freebies for your film club. That takes salesmanship. And coaching little league takes leadership and organization. Plus a ton of patience.

You see where I'm going with this. Obviously, what skills and experience you choose to highlight on your resume will depend on what jobs you're applying for. Even if something was only 10 or 20% of your job, it's worth mentioning it if you developed a skill or have experience that's relevant and transferable.

Want to take this idea from theory to practice? Think back to your work history from chapter two, where you listed all of your jobs, volunteer work, and activities. What skills did you develop and what experience did you gain in each of these jobs (even if it wasn't a huge part of the job) that might be transferable to jobs you'll apply for now? Try to think of at least two or three transferable skills for each job, volunteer gig, or activity. Write it down and find a way to pop that shiz into your resume.

Here's what I'm talking about: When I was a student, I had a part-time job as a resident assistant. If you've ever lived in a college dorm, you know what this is — the upper year student who is the unofficial big sister/peppy welcome wagon/rule enforcer on your floor. Unofficial big sister doesn't exactly seem legit enough to put on your grown-ass resume, but it *totally* is when you frame it in the right way. I was able to put things like community building, event planning, conflict management, and relationship development on my resume. I got promoted to team lead of the other resident assistants in my final two years of school, so I was able to talk about leadership and my experience with training and development. Suddenly seems kind of legit, right? Here are a few more examples from my own experience at graduation time to get you thinking about your transferable skills:

I was a reporter for a small-town newspaper one summer, and a production intern at a news network. Those gigs gave me awesome research and writing skills. Plus, an ability to work to quick deadlines.

I worked reception at the campus center for students with disabilities, and as a research assistant for a blind student. Those jobs gave me more research and administrative skills, as well as an education in diversity and inclusiveness.

I was a documentary producer for a big (albeit very amateur) school project. This gave me experience with project management, leading a team, and troubleshooting on the fly.

I worked a part-time job at a happy hardcore retail store (think trippy candles and body jewelry) and also at the front desk of a residence that turned into economy lodging in the summer (think one step above a hostel). I became a pro at customer service because of those gigs.

For a couple of weeks, I got to work at the head office for the retail store I worked at. Even though that was a very small part of my overall experience with that company, I was able to put things like product packaging and brand development on my resume.

School projects, part-time gigs, extracurriculars, volunteer work, summer jobs — literally EVERYTHING has some transferrable skills you can put on your resume. This was true for me, and it's true for you, too. If you look hard enough, you'll realize you have way more relevant experience than you thought you did. And you can get more . . .

➡ INTERNSHIPS ⬅

Internships can be awesome. They can help you get legit experience, develop some skills, build your resume, establish some career street cred, and get your foot in the door.

But some internships are the Netflix and chill of the career world — your interaction will be brief, anticlimactic, and unlikely to lead anywhere long-term. Which is totally fine if you're into that kind of thing.

Will you be an intern who gets coffee and spends your day making photocopies, or will you be an intern who goes to important meetings and makes a real contribution? Some organizations have interns who do the latter — the cool important stuff. And some organizations are looking for people who are DTF — definitely the former. (Get your mind out of the gutter!) The question is: How do you tell a promising internship from the Netflix and chill variety?

First you have to decide what you *want* out of your internship (if you even want one at all). Only then can you tell if it's the right internship for you.

What do you mean, "What do I want out of my internship?"
To get some legit work experience to put on my resume. Duh.

How do you tell a promising internship from the Netflix and chill variety?

Oh, honey, you can do so much better than that. There are lots of other things a person might want to get out of an internship. And different people want different things. Here's what I'm talking about:

- *I don't really care what it is, but it HAS to be paid. I am done with this student debt bullshit.*
- *I want to be able to put this super badass organization on my resume. Even if it means getting people coffee and working for free.*
- *I want to know what it's like to work for a start-up. I've heard it's supercool, but also really intense. I want to try it on.*
- *I've had my eye on this amazing company for a while, and this is a good way to get my foot in the door and show them what I've got.*
- *I went to school for applied physics, but I think I actually want to work in sales. This sales internship will help me figure out if it's a good fit.*
- *I didn't learn much about event management in school. This internship will help me learn more about that.*

- *This industry is all about who you know, so I'm gonna get in there and network like a mofo.*

When I was a career rookie, I did an internship with the news department of a national television station. I worked as an assistant field producer, which sounds somewhat sexy, but really what I did was a bunch of background research. I had no desire to be in front of the camera. I thought I'd like gathering information and coming up with stories, and so I wanted to try it on. And I secretly hoped that I'd love it, and kick ass at it, and it would turn into a real job.

An awesome end to this story would be if that had happened. But nope. I didn't like the work. AT ALL. Not only did I not like my work, I realized I had zero desire to work in news and television in general. The culture just wasn't for me. I didn't see that coming. I panicked because my career plan was now royally fucked, but I am SO grateful for that internship. I went in wanting to get some experience (I did) and to see if it was a good fit (it wasn't), and I got the information I needed (thank you, next).

So what do you want to get out of an internship? Think about it. And if internships aren't your jam, think about what you want out of an entry-level job. Same idea. A great gig will be easier to identify if you know what you're looking for.

If you're down with a Netflix and chill internship, that's fine (#notjudging). And if you're looking for something more, remember what you want and don't settle for less.

➡ SEVEN SECONDS OF GLORY ⬅

Nothing feels more career legit than talking about resumes and cover letters and even (gulp) LinkedIn profiles. Yes, we're going to go there, and no, it's not going to suck.

To be honest, a lot of resume and cover letter stuff is DRY. It's kind of a snoozefest by nature. So we're just going to talk about the super important stuff. And you can feel free to trawl the interwebs for the other stuff you need — resume templates, cover letter samples, whatever. That stuff is pretty easy.

You probably have a resume. Maybe you had to make one for a business communications class. Or maybe the nice lady at your college career center helped you make one. Or maybe you just made your own using a template on the internet . . . because, honestly, resumes are pretty basic.

Here's what happens to your resume after you apply for a job: It will almost always get screened by software that looks for the right keywords. No keywords? Sorry about your luck. That's why it's important to tweak your resume for every single job you apply for — you want to make sure you're using some of the same language as you see in the job description.

Next your resume will get thrown into a pile and given to the hiring manager. Or someone from HR. Basically, who-ever is in charge of the hiring. Then that person will spend seven seconds looking at your resume.

Seven seconds?! You must mean seven minutes.

Nope. Seven seconds. Literally. That's the average amount of time a resume gets at first glance. Your future boss is super busy and just wants to get a general sense of what she's dealing with before she puts your resume into one of two piles — keep or toss. You know which pile you want to be in, and that's why the following is so important . . .

➡ NO BORING SHIT ⬅

Do you have a little section called "objective" at the top of your resume, where you tell the reader you're applying for a job? BORING! Get rid of it. That's something people put in their resumes like 20 years ago. At some point, I guess people wised up to the fact that if people sent you their resume, they wanted a goddamn job. (You'd think that would be obvious.) Plus, you're going to say what job you're applying for in your cover letter.

And if your resume could be mistaken for a Tolkien manuscript, you have GOT to make some formatting changes. Paragraphs are dense and boring. Use bullets. And bullets should be no longer than two lines of text, by the way. One is even better. Keep it concise. No boring shit.

Basically, you want to make it super easy for the person reading your resume to see how awesome you are. That's why you use bullets instead of paragraphs. And that's why you use easy-to-read fonts and clear headings. And no redundant information. You want to make that sucker as easy and as pleasant to read as possible.

Same goes for your cover letter. And, yes, you need a cover letter. One that is tweaked and tailored for each job you apply for. Because your future boss can spot your lazy, generic, vanilla cover letter from a mile away. If you're submitting a generic cover letter, you might as well just send an email that says *I literally DGAF *shrug emoji**.

Cover letters are tricky. You need to tell your future boss how awesome you are without sounding like a douche. Do it in a non-boring way — in non-robotic, non-jargony language that an actual human might use in real conversation — and in about half a page (2/3 of a page max), and you're off to the races. You've just drastically increased your chances of going in the keep pile.

If you want to level up your resume but you don't know where to start, try adding a "Qualification Highlights" section at the top of your resume before you get into job-specific work experience. This section should be custom tailored for every single job you apply for (so should the rest of your resume, BTW, but this section *especially* so). Use this section to write four or five very short bullets that directly link your skills and experience to the top requirements of the job. For example, if you're applying for a job in IT at a retail organization, don't wait for your future boss to dig down to the middle of your resume to discover that you already have experience doing IT work for a retailer. Make one of your bullets "Retail IT specialist, experienced with point-of-sale and back system management," or whatever language is relevant from the job description. Remember, your future boss only looks at your resume for seven seconds the first time they pick it up, so put the super relevant stuff right upfront.

Another pro tip: Make it measurable. Numbers help you tell stories. Numbers are therefore sexy. Don't say you have "leadership experience." (Hello, vague!) Say you were the senior team lead for eight camp counselors, and were involved in hiring, training, and oversight of day-to-day operations. See? WAY BETTER. And don't say you have conference planning experience. Say you were the corporate sponsorship liaison for a conference with 500 attendees and increased sponsorship by 25% from the previous year. Boom. ASTRONOMICALLY more interesting.

What about a LinkedIn profile? You don't *need* one, but you might seem more legit if you have one. Your LinkedIn profile is resume-*ish*, but with more personality. You can list your work experience there, and you can also write up a little summary about who you are and what you care about. And you can link to portfolios and projects you've worked on. Have a little fun with it. I have a Muppet video and some artwork from my website on my LinkedIn page.

Take advantage of the headline section on LinkedIn. Introducing yourself as "Graduate of Mediocre Community College X" is way too boring. If people aren't at least somewhat intrigued by your headline, they're not going to keep reading. Get more specific about something you've done, or something you *want* to do. Something like, "City Planner.

Urban cyclist. Working hard to make your commute better."
Or "Software Architect. Let's build something together."
Or, depending on the industry you want to be a part of, you
might get away with adding in something a little cheeky, like
"Corporate Hippie. Environmental strategist. Passionate
about making you money while saving the planet." Or
"Digital Marketer | Sales Funnel Ninja | Facebook Ads
Wizard | Cat Dad."

Numbers help you tell stories. Numbers are therefore sexy.

After your headline, you can write a little summary.
You'd be nuts not to take advantage of this. It's your chance
to tell a little story about who you are, what you care about,
and why you're awesome. My own summary is three very
short paragraphs where I talk about my work as a career
coach, writer, and public speaker. Easy peasy. If you're just
starting your career, you might want to just write a couple
of interesting, punchy sentences. Also take advantage of the
media section, where you can link to videos or webpages or
portfolio samples or anything else that might be relevant to
your career. I link to my press clippings and my free online
career course (which you can find at careergasm.com).

Your LinkedIn page doesn't have to be a snoozefest; get
creative and show your personality! Just not *too* much personality, okay? Your profile pic shouldn't be a gym selfie.

Or a photo with Red Bull and vodka in the background. And, Jesus Christ, no duckface. No thirst traps. Nothing that involves you in a bikini on a pool float. Save it for Tinder. Keep if profesh, but also . . . no boring shit.

So grab that stale, vanilla resume of yours (and while you're at it, your cover letter and LinkedIn profile, too) and take a blowtorch to the boring bits. Get creative, be concise, and show a little personality. Speaking of showing personality, you know your potential employer is going to Google you, right? Up your privacy settings on social media and make sure all of your profile pictures are semi-respectable. You can thank me later.

✍ BYOB: WORKING FOR YOUR OWN DAMN SELF ✍

All of the stuff we've talked about so far in this chapter is going to be super helpful for you as you're getting ready to apply for jobs. But what if you want to work for yourself? What if you want to be your own boss?

The work world has changed pretty radically in the last 20 years or so. Hell, even in the last 10 years. Thirty-five percent of people are now doing some kind of freelance or entrepreneurial work — some of them are doing it full time, and some of them are doing it on the side.

Entrepreneurship is a mighty attractive option for many people. You can make up your own hours, there's nobody to answer to, and sometimes you can even work at home in sweatpants (which, admittedly, is what I'm doing right this very second). There's also a downside, of course. The learning curve is steep, there are no health benefits, your income is sporadic, and there's no guarantee that your business will be successful.

If you're considering starting your own business, there are a few questions you'll want to consider before you decide to go for it. Well, actually there are *several* questions you should consider — too many to list here — but this'll get you started:

HOW'S YOUR WORK ETHIC?

Working for yourself means you answer to nobody but yourself (well, except your customers and clients, but that's very different than answering to a boss). Are you organized? How's your time management? Are you self-motivated? Because if you usually need someone to crack the whip to get shit done, working for yourself might not be the best idea.

ARE YOU ANY GOOD?

Do you have skill and natural talent and knowledge to do good work in the area you want to build your business in? And if you *don't* have the right skills or knowledge yet, do you have a really solid plan for getting them? And do you have at least some experience?

ARE YOU GOOD AT THE *BUSINESS* SIDE OF BUSINESS?

Another thing to consider: It's not enough to just be good at the thing you're selling — art or personal training or web design or whatever — you also have to get really good at marketing and selling it (or have the cash to pay someone else to do that). Believe it or not, a lot of people forget about the *business* side of running a business (which, I know, sounds crazy, but it's true). Unfortunately, it's not enough to open up shop just because there's something cool that you like to do. You gotta have the chops for it. All of it.

HOW DO YOU FEEL ABOUT RISK?

Some businesses cost a lot of money to get off the ground. Are you cool with that? And even if the business you want to create has virtually no start-up cost (like working as a freelance copywriter or tutoring people online), are you cool with having an unstable income? And are you cool with giving your all to this business without knowing for sure if it will take off? Because even if you *do* have the work ethic and skill and talent and knowledge, it's still a gamble. That sucker can crash and burn. Or fizzle out before it even gets going.

> A lot of people forget about the *business* side of running a business.

I know what you're thinking. *Holy discouraging, Batman. Thanks for crapping all over my idea. Next time on* Shattered Dreams: *Sarah drops in on a kindergarten class and reveals who Santa REALLY is.*

Listen, I'm just trying to be real with you. And I'm not

trying to talk you out of entrepreneurship at all. Really. I just don't want you to pop up a business and sit back and wait for your Hollywood Walk of Fame star. I want you to be ready for everything that comes with it, so you don't get screwed.

Because despite all the heavy stuff I just mentioned, starting your own business and working for yourself can be AMAZING! It's what I did. And I help lots of other people do it, too, almost always using the *side-hustle* approach.

⇒ THE SIDE-HUSTLE APPROACH ⇐

A side hustle is a business you build on the side while you have another steadier job, and there are three main reasons why starting a biz this way (vs. going all in, balls to the wall from the very beginning) is an awesome way to go, especially at the beginning of your career.

1. CASHMONEY

If you're a recent graduate, my guess is you probably don't have a dump truck full of cash in your backyard just waiting to be invested in a business. In fact, there's a good chance that you have some student debt. Slowly developing your business while you work full time at another job that gives you a stable income will ensure that you're not living out of a shopping cart six months from now. I have a client who taught sewing classes while she built her business. And another who taught improv classes. One who was a bartender. One who worked reception at a float tank spa. Those jobs paid the bills while they were hatching their plans.

2. GETTING PAID TO LEARN

A super clever, very strategic option is to work a job that's related to the business you want to build. That way you can get paid to learn the stuff that will eventually make you more successful in your business. One of my clients took on contract work as a resume writer with a large organization before she took her own resume writing business full time. Another worked as a marketing strategist for a large company while he planned and built his own marketing agency. And one took a job merchandising at an existing retail store, so she could learn more about how product sourcing works — something that would eventually serve her in her own stationery business. Brilliant!

3. WORKING OUT THE KINKS

Here's something you ought to know: You're not going to come up with your business idea and knock it out of the park right away, or probably even in the first six months or year. That's especially true if you want to build a business in an area you don't have a ton of experience in yet. Having a nice, stable income coming in while you start your biz gives you time to work out some of the initial kinks. It gives you a chance to learn and adapt and correct some of that stuff, so your business can be in good shape before you ditch your job and take it full time. One of my clients worked for a telecommunications company while he built a consulting company. One worked in advertising while he worked on his furniture design business. One worked in a research lab while she slowly developed her meditation center. And while they had those safety nets, they worked out the kinks in their own businesses.

Taking the side-hustle approach can give you exactly the kind of time and financial support and even education you need to increase the odds of your business being successful. And of course you want your biz to be successful! Think of the high you'd feel from making something uniquely yours, putting it out into the world, and then having it take off. (It's incredible, let me tell you.) So if starting your own business is your dream, I say get after it, just be really *smart* about it.

9

INTERVIEWING LIKE A BALLER

So now you're a little clearer about what some of your career options are. And you've discovered you have more legit transferrable skills than you thought you did. And you're even stepping up your resume game. My friend, you're ready to get out there and apply for some jobs. So let's talk job interviews.

Just *thinking* about a job interview is enough to give most people hives. The stakes are high, and it can be pretty damn intimidating. Especially for a career rookie. So we're just going to work on a couple of things here to help you keep your cool. Let's talk about *preparing* vs. *practicing*.

For the love of god, don't practice your answers to interview questions. If you rehearse, you're going to sound like a robot. But you can *prepare*. Start by writing down any interview questions you think you might get that you're secretly dreading. For example, if the question "Where do you see yourself in 10 years?" makes you want to cry-scream, *"I HAVE NO FUCKING IDEA, SO STOP PRESSURING ME, MAN!!!"* you might want to put that on the list, so you can prepare for it.

For each question that freaks you out, come up with one or two bullet points you can talk about. Write something true (you shouldn't lie in an interview) and write *only* bullet points, just the gist. If you write out sentences, you'll sound rehearsed or, worse, you'll forget your exact wording, draw a total blank, and start to panic. And panicking doesn't exactly make for a stellar interview.

For example, for the dreaded 10 years from now question, you might just write something like:

- Not sure
- Corporate communications

That way when your interviewer asks where you want to be 10 years from now you'll be able to truthfully and naturally say, *"I'm not absolutely certain yet, but definitely something in corporate communications."* (Or whatever broad area you think you might be interested in.)

Or if your former boss was a militant asshole, and you dread the question "So why did you leave your last job?" you might write something like:

- Stronger leadership

That way you can say something honest but sufficiently vague, like, "I'd really like to work for someone with strong leadership skills who I can learn from. I didn't get that in my previous job." You didn't smack talk your old boss (A+ for professionalism), and your interviewer will probably read between the lines.

There are some interview questions you should always be ready for because they (or some version of them) are so damn common. Questions like:

TELL ME ABOUT YOURSELF. Make sure you actually have something ready to say, or you'll look like a possum caught in the headlights of an oncoming car and be off to a really shitty start to the interview. Try a mix of mostly professionally relevant stuff, with maybe one interesting personal detail thrown in.

WHAT'S A WEAKNESS OF YOURS? Don't give a douchey, bullshit answer like, "I'm a perfectionist." (Gag.) Say something you legitimately struggle with, and then (importantly!) how you remedy or work around this. For example, if time management isn't your forte, you might say something like, "I haven't mastered time management yet, so I'm working on it by being diligent about plotting all of my project timelines piece-by-piece in my calendar." Or let's say you're a little uncomfortable and awkward socially. You might want to say something like, "I'm rather shy and uncomfortable in new groups. I get around that by trying to have a two-minute conversation with somebody new every day. It forces me out of my comfort zone and helps me practice being social."

WHY DO YOU WANT THIS JOB? A good answer is an honest answer. But not brutally honest, okay? If you're applying for this gig just for the money, you can't say that. Make your answer related to something attractive about the job and (ideally) your career goals. Depending on what's true for you, you might say something like, "I hope to become a real estate agent myself in a couple of years, and I can learn a lot about the industry while providing administrative support for your real estate firm." Or "I really excelled at case studies in school, and I love being a part of a team. I know this is an entry-level position, but I'm excited about the tight-knit team environment here and the opportunity to play a role in executing the strategic vision for your clients."

WHY SHOULD WE HIRE YOU? This is related to — but a bit different than — the previous question. The last one was about what's attractive to you about the job. This one is about what makes *you* attractive to *them* as a candidate. Don't panic and say something vague and arrogant like, "I'm the best candidate." Not helpful. Get specific. Link your skills and experience to the things they've said are important parts of the job. You could say something like, "I understand that you're looking for self-motivated individuals who can work to tight deadlines. As I mentioned, I actually thrive in deadline-based environments and find

175

time-based project work highly motivating." Or something like, "I'm extremely detail-oriented. You've probably noticed that most of my work history is heavily focused on organization and detail work. I know that's an important quality you're looking for in this position."

A little preparation goes a long way. I mean, you wouldn't go on a first date without doing a thorough internet stalking of your date and planning a cute outfit, right? It's the same idea for job interviews: do a little research and prepare yourself, so you can look good when it counts.

➡ #OOTD ⬅

Let's talk about your Outfit of the Day. You probably feel like you've got this interview attire thing handled, but job interview outfit train wrecks happen to good people every day, so we can't let this topic slide. Let's just make sure you're on the right track, m'kay?

Don't worry, I'm not going to tell you that you have to hit up Boring Emporium of Responsible Attire, but you can't show up in a tube top, either. Same goes for your Not Here to Make Friends T-shirt. Not a good look. Same for high heels you can't walk in, anything that says Real Housewife, or that getup you wore to Coachella. Anything that might easily be mistaken as club gear or a costume is OUT.

I was a hiring manager in a former career, and here's

A little preparation
goes a long way.

some of the shit I saw walk (and occasionally stumble) into job interviews:

- More sweaty cleavage than a Friday night at the club
- Crusty flip-flops
- Ripped jeans. With BIG rips. In the crotch.
- Ass cheeks (psst . . . your skirt is too short)
- Smiley face underwear (psst . . . I can see through your white pants)
- Five-inch clear Lucite heels that are impossible to walk in
- Daddy's suit jacket that is three sizes too large
- Fake lashes so long that eye contact is a struggle
- Electric blue pit stains on bright blue shirts (Tip: if you're a sweater, stick to white or black)
- A strapless bridesmaid dress
- More leg than Angelina at the Oscars
- Belly buttons
- Hairy man belly buttons

In short, if you have to ask, "Is this outfit interview-appropriate?" the answer is probably no.

Do you have some interview gear? You should. You don't need a whole wardrobe, just one or two outfits. Because an interview might sneak up on you fast. Like, *not enough time to go shopping* fast. That's when people panic and try to pass off the miniskirt they wear clubbing as work-appropriate. Sexy corporate cosplay is out. Get it together and have a proper outfit ready. Your job interview is not a rom-com meet-cute where your future boss turns out to be your spin-class crush, hands you the job, and then asks you if you want to pop across the street for drinks.

> If you have to ask,
> "Is this outfit interview-appropriate?"
> the answer is probably no.

Not sure how people dress at the organization you're interviewing for? Depending on the place, it might be anything from jeans and sneakers to three-piece suits. My advice: Always err on the side of more formal. Assuming the dress code is more relaxed than it actually is will leave you feeling (and looking) schlubby in your interview. Not a winning strategy. Even if you're interviewing for a cool start-up and an insider friend tells you it's a chill dress code, it's never a bad idea to look slightly more polished, just in case. You know, something in the middle range between beachwear and full-length ball gown. A button-down shirt and some nice pants will almost always do the trick.

➡ JUST BE COOL ⬅

You're waiting in the lobby, feeling a little anxious about your interview but holding it together, when suddenly the receptionist pops in and says, "We're ready for you." Whew! Okay, time to show 'em what you've got. You can do this. But wait, you notice that everyone else in the lobby is getting up, too.

Shiiiiit. It's a group interview, and you didn't see it coming.

As you walk to the conference room, you spot the prom-queeny Malibu Barbie lookalike from your Psych 101 class out of the corner of your eye. Your inside voice is all like, *Come at me bro*, but outwardly you're as cool as avocado toast. You got this.

Group interviews are way more common than they used to be, and there are lots of things your future boss might be looking for in them, so it can be hard to prepare. Here are a few things to keep in mind:

SPEAK UP, BUT DON'T STEAMROLL. You want to be assertive, but not aggressive. You know that girl who always grabs the Bachelor first at the cocktail party? Don't be her. Be the first to answer a couple of questions, but if you steamroll your peers or monopolize everyone's time, you'll come across as pushy.

BE SPECIFIC. If the intimidation factor is causing you to panic and give two-word answers, try to be less vague in your responses. One handy trick is to add the words "for example" to the end of every answer you give (even if they didn't ask for an example), and then follow up with a little story that demonstrates what you just said.

Here's what I mean: If you get a question like, "Do you prefer to work in a team or individually?" you could just say "In a team." But that's a super boring answer. Instead try, "In a team. For example, in my last job I worked in a team of six people. I find my ideas are better when I can bounce them off people and collaborate. I also tend to learn more in a team because I can see how others do things differently." See how that's way more interesting? Saying "for example" forces you to tell a little story. And people love stories. Even little ones. They're much more interesting and engaging than dry, factual information. (Actually, building out your answers with "for example" is a good trick for traditional one-on-one interviews, too.)

DON'T THROW SHADE. Maybe you're interviewing with a group of idiots and assholes — like that one guy who always yells "Opa!" when someone drops a glass, and a bunch of people you're *certain* would have been sorted into Slytherin. Do not let your facial expression convey your judgy thoughts, whether the person next to you was just super rude or just said the most idiotic thing you've ever heard. Your body language says more than you think it does. Keep it in check.

BE MEMORABLE. Don't just shuffle out the door at the end of the interview with all of the other candidates. Hang back and offer up a handshake and a personal thank you to your interviewers. Then follow up with a same-day thank you email — something short, but with a little bit of personality. Maybe make a little joke (for god's sake make sure it's appropriate!) or refer back to something that came up in the discussion. At the very least, be warm and reinforce your excitement about the position.

Related to group interviews are panel interviews — where the tables are turned and there's a bunch of *them* and only one of *you*. When you face a panel of interviewers on your own, your anxiety may spike a little more than it would in a traditional interview. That's normal. Just remember to breathe, take your time, and remember to make eye contact with each of the interviewers when you give your responses, not just the one asking the question. The good news (and also, I suppose, the bad news) is that in a panel interview, you'll probably have a mixed bag of interviewer personalities — some friendly faces mingled in among a few crusty curmudgeons. If you get nervous or are thrown by a particularly tricky question, look to the person with the friendly, encouraging disposition until you're feeling solid again.

⇒ TWO-WAY STREET ⇐

Job interviews are how employers suss out the people they want to hire. But let's not forget that interviews are a two-way street. Interviews are also *your* chance to see if these guys are people you actually want to work for. And how do you do that? By paying attention and by asking questions.

Most people are so stressed about performing well in an interview that they forget to *pay attention*. You should pay attention for things that confirm the good stuff you want to hear and also be on the lookout for red flags. Here's what I mean:

Your interviewer casually mentions that some of the office crew are going out for sushi after work. *Cool. Sounds like the people who work here actually like each other.*

Your interviewer asks if you're available to work on evenings and weekends, and no, there's no overtime pay. *Red flag.*

The person interviewing you mentions that the person whose job you're applying for got promoted a year in, and that's why they're hiring. *Sweet. Upward mobility.*

Interviews are a two-way street.

Fail to pay attention, and you might miss those juicy little bits of information. But you shouldn't just pay attention in your interview; you should straight-up ask about the things you want to know. Fail to ask any questions and a) they won't think you're serious about the job, and b) you won't have the info you need to make a good decision about accepting a job offer.

Depending on the job, you may want to ask questions like:

- What will I do on a typical day?
- How many of your interns get hired on full time afterwards?
- Who will I be working most closely with?
- What roles do people tend to get promoted to from this position?

And any number of other questions. Except pay. You'll discuss pay when you get your job offer. We'll talk about that in the next chapter.

Make sure you have two or three interview questions ready to roll. If you ask none, you'll come off as apathetic. If you ask more than three, you'll come off as high-maintenance. This is probably your last chance to show them that you've really put some thought into things. Don't blow it in the home stretch; dazzle them with a sparkling finish.

⇒ EXPECT THE UNEXPECTED ⇐

Heads-up. You may have to interview in a less-than-ideal space or in a very impromptu, informal style. As I write this, there are two dudes beside me interviewing a recent grad in a bustling, very public lounge. The candidate is nailing it, BTW. She's just going with the flow with very general open-ended questions like "Tell me about yourself" and "Tell me about school," which aren't even really questions at all, but rather prompts for conversation. She's providing interesting, detailed little stories for each of her responses. And her body language and tone are comfortable and natural and professional despite the hectic setting. I wouldn't be surprised if she gets the gig.

Here are some other unexpected interview scenarios you might want to be ready for:

What if you have to interview on a big, cushy couch? Make sure your interview outfit works for a variety of settings, not just a boardroom table. For example, if you're thinking about wearing a skirt that might ride up, maybe go with pants. Or if your button-down shirt is a little too tight and might gape between the buttons if you're in a slouchy position, maybe go with something a little roomier. Could you be comfortable sitting on a tall stool? Standing? Walking and talking? Going up and down stairs? In a hot room? In a cold room? Be prepared for anything.

What if the interview goes really well, and you're invited to go on a tour of the office? Make sure you block off enough time after the interview in case it goes longer than you expect, either because they're running late, or there's a tour, or whatever. And again, make sure your outfit is appropriate. Wear comfortable shoes you can easily walk in. (Ladies, I know your five-inch stilettos are hot, but if you can't stomp in them easily and quickly, leave them at home.)

What if you get there and are expected to haul it to a coffee shop or restaurant? Maybe the boardroom your interviewer wanted to use is taken. Or maybe she hasn't had lunch yet and needs to grab some food, so you end up around the corner at Panera Bread. You gotta be ready to roll with weird location changes. Wear a professional-ish looking coat in case you unexpectedly find yourself having to walk around the block to Starbucks in the middle of February. And bring some cash, so you can buy your own latte.

What if the interviewer is totally unprepared for your arrival? Maybe their admin assistant failed to put the appointment in their calendar. Or maybe the person who was going to interview you is sick, and this person has to sub in. You have to be ready to drive the conversation and sell yourself if the person you expect to do that is unprepared. That means preparing in advance for the main points you'd like to get across and finding a way to steer the conversation in that direction. Also, always bring a few extra copies of your resume and cover letter just in case your interviewers don't have one.

Now you're truly interview-ready for ANYTHING, my friend. Get out there and shine!

10
MO' MONEY

You rocked your resume, nailed the interview, and snagged a job offer. So pop open some bubbly, your work here is done!!!

Um . . . not so fast.

It's time to negotiate your salary.

As a career rookie, it might not even occur to you to negotiate your salary. Most recent grads are so grateful just to be taken seriously and get a job offer that in their exuberance they simply say, *SWEET. Where do I sign?!*

If you've already done that, don't panic. You will have many more job offers throughout the course of your life, and you'll have the chops to negotiate your next one. Plus, what you're going to learn next will help you negotiate your first raise in your current gig, too.

So. Let's get down to business . . .

⇒ WEEKEND IN VEGAS ⇐

Some employers post salaries for the jobs they're hiring for, but you've probably noticed that most don't. I know, I know. This is extremely frustrating as a job applicant, especially if you're a career rookie. You have to do a lot of hoop-jumping — customizing your resume, writing the cover letter, attending the job interview (sometimes several rounds), and getting a job offer — before you even know if this mother-effing job is going to adequately support you.

Not only do you have to put in a ton of work upfront, but the whole process of negotiating your salary can be disorienting. For most career rookies, the first salary negotiation is like a rough weekend in Vegas — you leave stunned and feeling like a sucker, with way less money than you'd hoped, wondering, *What the hell just happened?!*

Let's make sure that doesn't happen to you.

If your potential employer has listed the salary with the job posting or has included a proposed salary with the job offer, AWESOME. That gives you a starting point to negotiate from and an idea of how much wiggle room you might have. You *could* simply accept the offer, or you could negotiate. I suggest the latter. Literally the worst thing that will happen is they'll say no, and then you'll have a decision to make. You won't have to feel resentful two or three years down the road wondering, *What if I had asked for more?*

If your potential employer hasn't listed the salary with the job posting or job offer, they're going to ask you one of two questions: *What are your salary expectations?* or *What was your previous salary?*

Literally the worst thing that will happen is they'll say no.

DO NOT FALL FOR THE SECOND QUESTION. It is a sketchy carnival game of a question (not to mention illegal in some places). Here's why: If you're a career rookie, your last job probably had a pretty shitty salary (if it was even salaried at all), amirite? By telling your future employer your previous (probably crappy) pay, you've just established yourself as a bargain-basement employee. They know exactly what you've accepted in the past and will presume what you'd likely be willing to settle for again. They'll be licking their lips like the Big Bad Wolf, ready to swoop in for a tasty little snack on the cheap. Big mistake, little piggy.

If you do get asked about your salary at your previous job, just dance around the question and reframe it as your current salary expectations. It's as easy at this . . .

THEM: What was your previous salary?

YOU: My salary expectation for this job is $_____.

They're just looking for a number. Or a range. And

frankly, what you've been paid in the past isn't relevant. (Especially if the job wasn't the same.) What you bring to the table *now* — and how you should be compensated for that — is what's relevant for *this* job.

⇒ THE PRICE IS RIGHT ⇐

There's this cheesy game on *The Price Is Right* that reminds me of salary negotiation. It's called Cliff Hangers, and like most games on *The Price Is Right*, the name of the game is to price an item as close to its retail value as possible. As the contestant is pricing the item, a little cardboard mountain climber climbs a little cardboard mountain slope at a 45-degree angle to the sound of yodeling music. If the price the contestant gives is in the right range, they win the prize, but if the price they give is too high, their little yodeling mountain climber falls off the cliff. Salary negotiation is like that, too. You have to name your price and hope that you don't fall off a cliff if you miss the mark.

Whether your future employer has offered a proposed salary with your job offer or is expecting you to offer one, you need some basic information in order to negotiate your salary wisely. You need to know two main things: what you want to be paid, and what the market salary range is for that job. And hopefully the former falls within the range of the latter. Less likelihood of asking for a salary that's way off the mark and falling off a cliff.

Some employers have tiered salary ranges that are published. This is often the case for government jobs, union jobs, and some industries that are heavily regulated. You may be able to dig up those salary ranges if you look hard enough. The levels will be listed by number or letter, with the higher numbers and letters listing salary ranges that are progressively higher. For example, one of my first legit grown-up jobs was an entry-level job that lists a starting salary of $50,500 to $60,000. As with that job, the higher end of most salary ranges is typically reserved for people who are experienced and have been in the job for several years.

If you can find a published salary range, your negotiation is going to be super easy because you know what's typical. If you're just starting out and don't have a ton of experience, ask for something in the middle of the range, so you'll have some wiggle room to negotiate down if they don't accept your first offer.

If you can't find a published salary range, you're not off the hook. In fact, most jobs won't have published salary ranges, so your negotiation pregame requires a little more digging and some number crunching. You may want to see what kind of salary info you can dig up about your employer on websites like Glassdoor, Salary, GetRaised, Indeed, Vault, TheJobCrowd, and similar platforms that encourage people to anonymously post information about their employers. There's no guarantee that you'll find anything, but if you do, it could inform your decision.

After you've gathered as much information as you possibly

can, it's time to come up with your number. Some people prefer to come up with a range. That's fine, too. Here are some questions you should consider when you come up with your number:

DOES WHAT YOU'RE ASKING FOR SEEM MARKET-APPROPRIATE BASED ON THE INFORMATION YOU'VE BEEN ABLE TO GATHER? If not, they

won't take you seriously. If you weren't able to find information about the exact job at your exact organization, try getting salary info for similar jobs at similar organizations. Have these numbers with you when you negotiate. They'll come in handy because you'll be able to demonstrate knowledge about the market, and the pressure will be on them to step up.

If you ask for an amount that is astronomically high compared to the market, you'll seem delusional and out of touch. If you ask for too little, you'll come across as unqualified and unfamiliar with the market. Yes, asking for too little can be a bad thing, not just for you but also for *them*. I overheard a salary negotiation in a coffee shop the other day. (I know. Awkward!) A woman was asked what her salary expectations were, and she said $30,000. The interviewer balked and said, "Is that enough to make you excited to come to work every day?" Awkward silence. Womp womp. The damage was done. The interviewer had already assessed her as inexperienced, and the conversation went downhill from there.

IS THIS A PURELY SALARIED JOB, OR ARE THERE OPPORTUNITIES FOR COMMISSIONS AND BONUSES? This could make a big dif-

ference in the salary you ask for. Especially if you're able to gather information about how much typical bonuses and commissions are for people in your job. It's okay to go ahead and ask for this information outright once you have the job offer. They'll be expecting you to factor potential bonus and commission income into your decision. This is obvious, but something to keep in mind is that salary is guaranteed while commissions and bonuses are based on performance. How this might impact your decision is entirely subjective. Some people get all squirrely just thinking about the uncertain nature of performance-based income, and for others it's highly motivating. You do you.

I recently had a conversation with a young woman who was nervous about asking for a signing bonus. She had received a great job offer, but her start date meant that she'd miss out on her annual bonus at her existing job . . . and it was a significant chunk of change.

"Can I ask for a signing bonus?" she asked. "We've already discussed salary, and it's generous, but I haven't signed yet. Is it too much to ask?"

I told her to express enthusiasm for the offer, explain that she'd like to accept it, but it would mean not receiving her bonus of \$___, and ask for a one-time signing bonus for that same amount. (I mean, the worst thing they could do is say no, right?) She took my advice, and I received an excited email from her the following week saying she'd gotten everything she'd asked for. If you don't ask, you'll never know. So you gotta ask.

> If you don't ask, you'll never know.
> So you gotta ask.

WHAT OTHER FORMS OF PERKS AND COMPENSATION ARE INCLUDED?

I'm talking about things like health benefits, extra vacation time, flextime, the ability to work from home, gym memberships, wellness plans, stock options, pension contribution matching, and even things like moving allowances and tuition reimbursements. I know that's a lot to think about as a career rookie, but you can (and should) ascribe a dollar value to each of these things based on what it's literally worth in dollars (as in the case of things like health plans, stock options, pension contributions, and tuition reimbursements), whether you'll actually use it (a moving allowance, gym membership, and discounted childcare are of no value to you if you're not moving, don't go to the gym, and don't have kids), and how personally important certain perks are to you (as in the case of extra vacation time).

A seemingly great-paying job might not seem so badass compared to a job that pays a little less but has killer benefits. You'll have to crunch the numbers to see how valuable those benefits are to you.

I once worked for an employer that paid for 100% of most health expenses, including things like vision, dental, and massage therapy. Unlimited massage therapy! That's like a free pass to the spa! Plus they matched pension plan contributions *and* had a generous tuition reimbursement program. My first master's degree was paid for almost entirely on their dime. Another employer not only paid for health basics, but also had a generous employee wellness plan that included options like a yoga studio membership, meal delivery, and house-cleaning. It was AMAZING.

Make sure you factor the subjective value of perks and benefits into your salary negotiation. And, for goodness sake, after you negotiate and have a deal, get that shiz IN WRITING. All of it — the salary, commission and bonus potential, every perk and benefit, vacation time, and everything else you've discussed. A promise is not the same thing as a contract.

🡆 GAME TIME 🡄

Here are a few final tips to help you make the most of your salary negotiation . . .

● MAKE IT ABOUT YOUR VALUE.

It's your job to make a convincing argument about what you bring to the table. If you get asked why they should pay you more than their initial offer, don't panic and say something like, "I have student loans!" Never talk about why you *need* the money. That's not a very empowered angle. It makes it seem like you're asking them to do you a favor. Focus on the value you bring — what they can get from *you*, not what you can get from *them*.

COUNTEROFFER.

When a potential employer gives you a job offer with a proposed salary, you can (and often should) counter their offer. You probably won't have to do this in person because you'll likely get your written offer via email. (But be ready, just in case!) Whether you're countering the offer in person, via email, or over the phone, first express your enthusiasm at having received an offer, then reinforce the value you bring (which hopefully you've already discussed at length in your interview), and then ask for more. Make it a specific number or a range with the low end comfortably higher than their initial offer. If they understand that you want the gig and will bring a lot of value and are being reasonable, they may be willing to go to bat on your behalf and work out a higher salary.

TRY TO DEFER SALARY NEGOTIATION UNTIL YOU HAVE A JOB OFFER IN WRITING.

You may get asked what your salary expectations are right in the job interview. This is not ideal because you likely don't know enough about the job to give them a well-informed number yet. If they ask for your salary expectations too early, try saying something like, "I'd like some more information about the specifics of the job so I can give you a well-informed number." They may press you. In that case, make sure you ask all the questions you need to know about the job itself and any perks and benefits before you give them a number.

REMEMBER, YOU CAN WALK AWAY.

Don't accept any job offer you'll resent, even when you're first starting out. Negotiating your salary before you accept a job is easier to do than negotiating a raise after you start, so don't accept a salary that will make you hate your life while crossing your fingers that you can negotiate an enormous raise in a year. Not likely. If you're not happy with their offer, or if they outright reject your counter-offer and don't come back with an acceptable number, that means you have a tough decision to make. Accepting or rejecting a job offer is a very personal, very subjective decision because of all of the stuff we've talked about. It's your call and yours alone.

If you decide to walk, do it with grace. Express interest in the job, enthusiasm for having received an offer, and then restate the number you need in order to accept the offer. You might say something like this: "I'm thrilled to be the chosen candidate, and I'm very interested in the job, but in order to accept the offer I would need $___. If that's not feasible, I understand, and I hope our paths cross in the future." No begging. No duking it out. Just transparency about what you need. They'll either meet you at your number, or you'll move on. The world is small. Stay classy.

• DON'T FREAK OUT IF THEY WON'T NEGOTIATE.

Some employers might find it straight-up surprising that you want to negotiate your salary, especially as a career rookie. And some organizations simply do not negotiate salaries — the salary presented to you in your job offer simply is what it is. Don't let that throw you off. If and when you counteroffer, they might simply say the salary is non-negotiable. No biggie. That just means you have to decide to take it or leave it. It's not personal. You usually won't find out if a salary is negotiable or not until you make a counteroffer, so don't feel weird about it if that's the case. It's still worth putting it out there.

➡ ASKING FOR A RAISE ⬅

Negotiating your starting salary is good practice for negotiating what you want in other areas of your career, too, like the projects you want to work on, time off, flextime, and of course promotions and raises. The earliest you should ask for a raise is typically one year in. If you've been killin' it at work for longer than that, it's appropriate to ask for a raise. Again, the name of the game is demonstrating value. You are not entitled to a raise just because you've put in the time, so put together a convincing argument for the increased value you're bringing compared to when you first started. Be as specific as possible, and try to be quantitative instead of qualitative. For example, instead of simply saying you "increased event

The world is small.
Stay classy.

enrollment," say you "increased event enrollment by 15%." Numbers help bolster your case. And make sure you get your timing right! Don't spring this on your boss when they're in a pissy mood, or when they're swamped. Book a meeting.

Maybe the nature of your job has changed significantly since you started, and a change in compensation is needed. Or perhaps you're being offered a promotion. I was once offered a "promotion" that was essentially a title change and more work but hardly any more money. I told my boss that it made more financial sense for me to stay in my existing job since I'd be doing more work for less money if I accepted the offer. There was no playing hardball, no poker face, just two women sharing information. She wasn't trying to screw me over, she just hadn't thought it out fully. Once I put forward my case, she found a way to get me more money, I accepted the promotion, and we were both happy.

➡ HEY LADIES ⬅

A guy I know — I'll call him Jack — shared the news of his promotion to me one evening. He had been working a contract gig and wanted to stay on a more permanent basis. So he worked up the nerve to set up a meeting with his boss. He got what he wanted, but in the process of meeting with his boss, Jack found out some interesting information. His boss *had* planned to give the promotion to Jack's colleague, Jill. But since Jack took the initiative to ask, *he* got it instead.

On the one hand, I was happy for Jack. But on the other hand — sigh — *how typical*. To this day, poor Jill probably has no idea that her promotion was swiped out from under her by a dude who was no better than she was at her job but simply found the guts to ask. And props to Jack and every other guy (and gal) like him! You *should* ask for what you want. But men typically ask for more, and ask more often, while women typically wait to receive things based on merit. I gotta ask, how's that workin' for ya, ladies?

This negotiation thing is tougher for us women. For several reasons. Many of which I will not get into because that could be a whole other book. (In fact, entire books *have* been written on this topic. Read them. Maybe start with *Women Don't Ask* by Linda Babcock and Sarah Laschever. *Feminist Fight Club* by Jessica Bennett is also fabulous and covers far more than just negotiation.) We live in a world that (still) socializes women to be nice, to be grateful, and to not be too assertive, or people might not like you. Which, as it turns out, is actually true. Study after study shows that men who assert themselves are perceived as strong while women who assert themselves in the same way are perceived as pushy and abrasive. There are double standards (many of them subconscious) for men and women, so women tend to get doubly screwed when it comes to salary negotiation. Because of differences in gender socialization, women are typically more apprehensive to ask for as much as men (or to negotiate at all). Again, study after study demonstrates this. Plus, when women *do* ask (no more or no less assertively than

202

men), they are perceived as pushy and abrasive. It feels like a damned if you do, damned if you don't situation.

Unfortunately, deep-rooted systemic issues like this don't have quick or easy solutions. So while this double standard is wildly unfair, not to mention a huge pain in the ass to navigate, it's going to take a good long while to change. And in the meantime you need to get paid. That means the best option is to ask for what you want. Despite any apprehension to do so, and despite any negative perceptions people may have of you for doing so. Nobody is going to hand it to you if you don't ask.

11
WERK IT

et's jump forward and assume you score a really awesome job. Maybe it's not your ultimate dream job yet, but hey, you're in the game. As you settle into your new job, enjoy it! Get to know the people you work with. Join your colleagues for lunch on Taco Tuesday. Sign up for the office ultimate frisbee team. Revel in the glory of unlimited access to all the pens, highlighters, and sticky notes you could ever want. But also . . . keep your eye on the prize.

The prize is you building a feel-good career — one you actually enjoy. It's doing work you like, continuing to learn and grow, and eventually taking home a bigger paycheck than you do now. Though, honestly, making a fuckload of money is overrated. There are a lot of people out there who have a ton of cash and hate getting out of bed on Monday morning.

Sure, go for that money, honey. More power to you. Just be sure you're making it doing something you like, okay?

Here's how you enjoy the job you have while keeping your eye on the prize: You get clear on how you want to *learn* and *grow* in your work. That's what we're going to do now. And there's no need for you to know exactly what your ultimate dream job is for you to decide how you want to learn and grow.

One of my clients — I'll call her Laura — wanted to develop her people skills. She worked for her dad's company, and she knew she could get away with acting bristly and entitled because she was the boss's daughter. Zero repercussions. So Laura took another job (at a company not run by her relatives) to force her to develop better people skills. Is that awesome or what?! First of all, admitting that your interpersonal skills kind of suck takes a lot of guts. And putting yourself in a new situation where you're forced to work on that stuff takes even *more* guts. A+ for her.

Another client — I'll call him Greg — wanted to develop more confidence. He was always afraid to speak up and share his ideas. This was a problem none of his colleagues seemed to have. He was waiting to magically develop confidence, but didn't realize that action precedes confidence, not the other way around. So, with a series of manageable baby steps, we had Greg test the waters and share his ideas more and more until confidence was no longer an issue.

Another client always feels the need to pretend he has the answers, so he wants to develop a level of comfort admitting when he doesn't know something. Another wants to learn how to better manage her anxiety at work. Another is trying to learn more about sales, and another about setting better boundaries. One has mega authority issues and wants to learn how to deal with that.

Everyone wants to learn and grow differently because everyone has different interests, different strengths, and different "areas for improvement."

Action precedes confidence, not the other way around.

What are some of the ways you want to learn and grow at work? They might be in areas that are obviously related to your career, like learning more about sales; or they might be in areas of personal development, like developing confidence or managing anxiety; or in areas that seem to straddle both your personal and professional lives, like learning how to set boundaries or admit when you don't know something or deal with authority figures.

Looking for opportunities to work on that stuff will definitely help you keep your eye on the prize. But do you know what one of the best ways to learn is?

➥ FUCKUPS ◄

Allow me to take the mystery out of this for you. As you continue to learn and grow in your career (and in life), you are going to make mistakes. OF COURSE you are going to make mistakes. Who do you think you are, Queen Bey herself?

You're going to do some stuff that isn't quite right. Sometimes you're going to miss the mark a little. Or a lot. Either way, no biggie. It's a part of being human, and you'll keep making mistakes until the day you die. If you're not fucking up occasionally, you're not growing. It's what you *do* with your fuckups that matters.

Most people are so embarrassed by their mistakes or so pissed at themselves for screwing up that they forget to pay attention to the *lesson*. Yes, the lesson. Every fuckup bears fruit that you can use to do better next time. If you can get out of your head and pay attention, you'll learn.

Exhibit A: In one of my first grown-up jobs, I had a colleague who was taking credit for my work. One day I had just HAD IT, so I went to my boss and angry-cried my way through an explanation of this injustice. My boss looked blankly at me and told me I should consider therapy.

One the one hand, *little harsh*, *Gretch*. But on the other hand, I probably shouldn't have lost my shit like that. Lesson learned. I wasn't necessarily wrong to tell my boss, but I should have done my crying in a bathroom stall like a respectable professional and chosen a better moment to have

207

a conversation with my boss. Or, even better, I should have confronted the person who was taking credit for my work. Calmly. Without going all *Game of Thrones* on her ass. I've never angry-cried over a boss's desk since then, and, fingers crossed, I never will again.

Exhibit B: I got fired once. Well, nobody technically used the words "you're fired," but the company I worked for suddenly "didn't need me" anymore. Right after I'd done something kind of stupid. So, you know, same difference.

As a student, one of my summer jobs was working for a radio station publicity team. Basically, I got to drive around in a boss SUV and give away free stuff at events in the city. One day, me and my publicity partner were driving around, and I spotted a nice area I thought would be cool to use. She disagreed.

Her: "I'm pretty sure that's private property. We can't do that."

Me: *Proceeds anyway*

It turns out it *was* private property, and the owner (understandably) wasn't impressed that we just rolled up and set up shop. When I called my boss for my hours the following weekend, I was told they didn't need me that weekend. Or next weekend. Or for the rest of the summer. It would have been so easy for me to just double-check if the property was public or private, but instead I was facing the consequence of a stupid mistake. Lesson 1: Sometimes your colleagues are right and you're wrong. Lesson 2: It never hurts to double-check.

Exhibit C: I burned a lot of money unnecessarily when I first started my career-coaching practice. I was eager to get started and keen to get my website built. Unfortunately, I didn't do enough research before I hired a company to do it. The company I hired did a custom-build, which sounds really fancy, but the way they did it meant that I couldn't adapt or edit any of the pages myself, which meant that I either had to live with a static website or pay through the nose to have them do every miniscule edit. I paid thousands of dollars and eventually had to abandon it and start all over and build a new website with someone else. Lesson 1: Don't jump into big decisions prematurely. Lesson 2: Do your research.

Now it's your turn. Take one of your career fuckups (it's okay, everybody has them) and look for the lesson. I'll get you started . . .

THE FUCKUP	THE LESSONS
Angry-crying to my boss	• don't address touchy subjects in an overly emotional state
	• when an issue arises, address the person directly involved
Trespassing in a company car	• maybe listen to what your colleague has to say
	• it never hurts to double-check
Hiring the wrong web designer	• don't rush into a big decision
	• do your research

If you're not
fucking up occasionally,
you're not growing.

Use the fuckup/lesson strategy to make the most of your mistakes at work. Cuz you're gonna make mistakes. You might as well learn from them.

One of my clients, Mark, gets extremely frustrated when trying anything new. He gets angry if he doesn't nail it right away. On top of that, he has unreasonably high standards (for others, but also for himself), and he has trouble asking for help. As a result, learning new things is difficult for Mark. He tends to only try things he knows he'll knock out of the park, and when he does stray from his comfort zone, he gets frustrated and self-critical really early in the process and abandons the project before he's over the learning curve. And if it's not something he knows he can master on his own, he won't even consider trying it.

> Getting harsh and judgy with yourself,
> or getting all defensive, is how you
> miss the lesson.

There's one thing that can really get in the way of learning, and it's the belief that you are not allowed to make mistakes. Getting harsh and judgy with yourself, or getting all defensive, is how you miss the lesson. Like when Mark beats himself up for not nailing something on the first try. Or when you have a code-red meltdown when a colleague points out some statistical errors in your report. Or when you find yourself day-drunk on boxed wine because you didn't get the promotion. Or when you freak out over that one little "room for improvement" evaluation on your performance review.

Repeat after me: I'm human, and making mistakes is a part of being human. Trial and error (and let's not forget that *error* part) is what helps you learn.

⫸ MENTORSHIP BY STEALTH ⫷

Now that you know what you want to learn, *who* do you want to learn from? Sure, you can do a little learning on your own from classes and the internet and trial and error, but other people — actual people living in the real 3-D world — will probably be your biggest source of learning. You need mentors.

Maybe you could ask one of the top sales reps in the company if you could shadow a couple of her sales calls. Maybe you could take your cousin out for beers and ask how he negotiated his salary. Maybe you could ask a seasoned coworker for a one-on-one meeting so you can do a run-through of your pitch. Or invite a senior colleague out for lunch to ask about how you might approach a difficult conversation with a client.

Asking for mentorship kinda feels like asking someone out on a first date. There's a certain level of awkwardness and vulnerability involved. It's still worth it. Do it. But you can also make someone your mentor without them even knowing. Sneaky, right? There's the watch-and-learn variety of mentorship — mentorship by stealth — where you just pay super close attention to how someone you respect and admire handles themselves. Pay attention to how she gives a presentation or collaborates with others (or whatever it is you want to learn to do better), and take notes. Okay, don't *literally* watch her and take notes, or loiter like a vampire waiting to swoop in for the kill. But you know what I mean. Watch and learn.

If you're not a part of a formal mentorship program and feel weird about straight-up asking for mentorship, consider mentorship by stealth.

Asking for mentorship kinda feels like asking someone out on a first date.

I had two amazing mentors in one of my first jobs after school. The first was a woman in a senior leadership position. She always spoke up, asked hard questions, and took the reins. But she was also the kind of leader who could see potential in others and would empower them to try things. I learned a lot about the kind of leader I wanted to be just by watching her. Another mentor at that same place taught me not to take myself too seriously. She was brilliant and powerful and knew how to get shit done, but she was also playful. She kept a voodoo doll in her office, and if I would come in fuming about something an idiot colleague had done, she would jokingly ask if I wanted her to break out the voodoo doll. She showed me how to cut the tension and lighten up, and how to take things less seriously.

I used to work as a professor, and I had great mentors in my academic career, too. Laurie was a professor who busted her ass and killed it in her field. She was a powerhouse. But she was also incredibly soft and kind. I often went to her for advice when I had a hard decision to make, and I always left her office feeling 100 times better than when I'd walked in. Simon was another incredible mentor. He was older, a few decades into his career in academia, and in many ways he was a bit of a rebel. His colleagues would bitch and moan (or brag) about spending the weekend working on a study or preparing a paper for publication, but Simon had really good boundaries between his work life and personal life — as in, he actually *had* a personal life. He spent his evenings and weekends seeing his zillion friends, doing mixed martial arts, and going to parties. His weekends were full of *fun*, not *work*, which if you ask me is exactly how it should be. I learned a lot about boundaries and healthy rebellion against burnout culture from him.

If you don't have any mentors in your immediate proximity, you're not off the hook. You'll have to make an effort to actually meet some, which means . . .

⇒ NETWORKING ⇐

Sorry if you just puked a little bit. Nothing triggers the ol' gag reflex like the word "networking." If you have an aversion to the idea of networking, it's probably because you're imagining a sweaty, coked-out, business card–dispensing douchebag getting all up in your grill. We've all met that guy. And your response is probably the same as mine — *Get the fuck away from me, dude*. So you pretend there's someone you know across the room and then make a run for it. But the truth is the shady d-bag types are usually the exception and not the rule.

So just put down your phone for a second and talk to the person sitting beside you when you're at a conference. Oh, you learn she's just started managing her own team, and that's something you hope to do one day. Sweet. Might be worth chatting her up. Or, if she's a total snob, you can just both go back to wasting time on your phones. Whatever. No big loss. The next time you hear the word "networking," I want you to think "conversations with people who might be cool, but you won't know until you talk to them."

There are lots of ways to network. And as an introvert who doesn't generally enjoy hanging with strangers, I can tell you they don't all suck. Networking doesn't have to mean working a room full of strangers. It might be talking to someone while you wait for the elevator. Or ditching the last conference session of the day to grab coffee with the cool chick you just met. Or having lunch with a colleague you don't know very well yet.

So what kind of people do you want to meet? I really like talking to other people who are doing similar work to me — other entrepreneurs, specifically other entrepreneurs who are a few steps ahead of where I am in my business. I like chatting up other service-based entrepreneurs who are a little further along than me in their journey. I find it inspiring, and I always learn something.

Let's also think about *how* you like to meet and connect with people. Some people love big events and meeting lots of people at once. Not me. Large groups of people give me a headache. Literally. If I'm at a large event, I'll kind of ignore most of the crowd and just have longer conversations with a handful of feel-good peeps — often other introverts who are working the same angle as me. (You'll find us by the food table or hiding in the corner.) Longer, deeper one-on-one conversations. That's my preferred networking vibe.

There are lots of ways to network — they don't all suck.

What's your networking vibe? Do you love large events and big groups of people? Small groups? Chatting one-on-one? Do you like structured interactions like icebreaker games or more organic interactions? Do you like to be introduced to people or hang as a part of a group or venture out on your own? How do you like to meet and talk to others? Getting clear on that will help to remove the ick factor from networking, so you can do it in a feel-good way.

If you keep this stuff up — the intentional growth, learning from your fuckups, seeking out mentors, and net-working — you're going to learn a lot. Quickly. You'll know the lay of the land, the rules, and how to rock that shit. But don't clutch your rule book too tightly. I also want you to embrace . . .

⟹ YOUR INNER ANARCHIST ⟸

There are people who play by the rules, get 'er done, and do a mighty fine job. Nothin' wrong with that. And there are also people who read the rule book, nod politely, and then BLOW. THAT. SHIT. UP. Workplaces are filled with rule breakers, and many of them are wildly successful. Which is why you should embrace your inner anarchist. At least occasionally.

Don't let those sensible button-down shirts and ortho-pedic shoes deceive you — Angela from accounting knows how to SLAY. She's only 25, but she had a radical idea that saved the company a shit-ton of money. So they gave her a massive bonus. And a promotion.

And instead of fucking around on Reddit for hours and hours like his colleagues, Nate put together a slick pitch to give the company's new line some killer publicity. Even though that's not his job. And now he gets to represent the company on national TV.

And while most people were afraid to make eye contact with the CEO, Jasmine, the new intern, chatted her up on the elevator and told her about an idea she had for the new launch. So she got invited to the next board meeting. And she's *just* an intern.

Stepping outside of the norm helped all of these people rise high and fast. Sometimes disregarding the rules is an awesome way to get ahead. Of course, that kind of thing can also get you fired, so just don't be a moron about it. (No getting drunk at work. No inappropriate shit. No embezzling funds. Be cool.)

Workplaces are filled with rule breakers, and many of them are wildly successful.

One of my favorite rebels is Alicia Keys. At the height of her music and TV career, she was just like, *You know what? There's this stupid rule I'm not gonna follow anymore. I'm done wearing makeup.* Maybe that doesn't sound very radical to you, but I find it wildly inspiring. It reminds me that there are things I can choose to opt out of. I love makeup, but I hate high heels, so I opted out of them. I haven't worn them in almost a decade — even when going on television or giving a keynote talk. I don't even own a pair anymore.

Another rule breaker I love is Martha Beck. She's a brilliant life coach and spiritual badass. And she's hilarious and neurotic and wise. After completing not one, not two, but *three* Harvard degrees, she was like, *Nope. This lifestyle is making me miserable. Imma switch it up. Peace out.* She's now living a deeply intuitive, more unstructured, and I would even say whimsical life while still drawing from her scientific roots. She's a wild, new-agey, intellectual hippie. She reminds me that we're all multifaceted, and that none of us has to be just one thing, but that we can choose to rock the different dimensions of ourselves.

Maybe you love how Elon Musk is all *Just watch me, bro* whenever somebody tells him something can't be done. You love that highly focused bravado and entrepreneurial spirit. You'd love to flex that in more of your work, actually. And maybe build something of your own.

Maybe you love Sarah Silverman's tell-it-like-it-is attitude. And how celebs like Mindy Kaling and Amy Schumer and Chrissy Teigen keep it real. People are always dancing around issues at work, and you'd like to just speak plainly and get things onto the table.

Think about all the rule breakers that inspire you and why. Then figure out how you can borrow from their playbooks and get out there and stir it up.

12

ARE WE THERE YET?

S o you've got an idea of the general direction for your career (or a few options), and you've got yourself a loose plan. But instead of celebrating this, it's possible that you're freaking out because you're not there yet. Amirite?

Remember going on a family road trip when you were a kid? You were excited just thinking about it. You'd get to go to a cool new place, and there would be things to see, and fun and adventure, and, best of all, CAR SNACKS!

But your sweet little seven-year-old self forgot that it would take awhile to get to the cool new place, and instead of enjoying the ride, you sulked about how long it was taking. You threw a fit of despair, asking in your most annoying, whiniest voice possible, *Are we therrrrre yet?* Every. Five.

Minutes. This does not make for a fun road trip, my friend. Not then and not now.

One of the most common things for people to say when they're trying to figure this career stuff out is *I feel like I'm already so behind*. And so my question is: Behind who? Behind people like your parents who've already been working for three decades? Yeah, you're about three decades behind them. Behind your older sister who has an awesome job she loves? Yeah, but that's just because she had a massive meltdown of her own after she graduated, and then she figured some things out and got her act together. Just like you're doing now.

Answer me this: Were you the kind of kid to get your test paper back, realize you did pretty good, but then immediately steal a glance at your friend's paper only to learn that she did even better? Kinda took the joy out of your own victory, didn't it?

There's a reason why no graduation speech in the history of ever has been titled Six Quick and Easy Steps to Kill It in Your Career and Get Everything You Ever Wanted. You know why? Not possible. That speech would be filled with lies. Because life is messy. So is work.

Slow down and take a breath. This stuff takes time to figure out. There's no need to rush to the finish. In fact, if you're thinking of your career as the finish line — a place where you can lean back and put your feet up once you get it all figured out — think again. Sure, there will be moments when you can enjoy the fruits of your labor, but for the most part, it's going to be in constant motion. There is no finish line.

No graduation speech in the history of ever has been titled Six Quick and Easy Steps to Kill It in Your Career and Get Everything You Ever Wanted.

⇒ CHECK THE BOX ⇐

If you're like me (ambitious and kind of a control freak), you probably wish your life could be organized into a set of clear-cut check boxes — a list of items you could check off quickly and efficiently until you reach the point where you can just relax, when you can finally say, *Welp, now that I've got that done, I can go ahead and enjoy my life*. You think to yourself, *I'll be happy when I . . .*

- *Move out of my mom's basement*
- *Have a sweet condo downtown*
- *Pay off my student loans*
- *Find my one true bae*
- *Score myself an awesome job*
- *Make a six-figure salary*
- *Shed those last five pounds*

- *Drive a sweet-ass sports car*
- *Obtain general baller status*

And the list goes on.

If you've been telling yourself the *I'll finally be happy when* _____ story, let me stop you right there. Pursuing your goals is awesome, but the payoff isn't some crazy pinnacle where you can just bask in the glory of it all. So there's no need to rush.

Are there some things you're frustrated you don't have yet or haven't accomplished yet? Take a sec and think about it.

Now, there are probably some totally legit reasons why you don't have that stuff yet, reasons why you're not there yet. For example, if you're frustrated that you haven't paid off your student loans, a totally legit reason for not having done that yet is that you just graduated awhile ago. That shit takes time. And if you're frustrated that you haven't scored an awesome job, a totally legit reason for not having done that yet is because you had to take some time to figure out what you want, and then even more time to actually get it.

It seems kinda silly that you'd expect to have all that stuff instantly, right? Pace yourself.

Something that takes the sting out of not being there yet is focusing on smaller chunks of time. Setting long-term goals is great, but it can sometimes feel frustrating because it takes so freaking long to achieve them. So let's pick a shorter time frame and just decide what's good enough *for now*. What could you be happy achieving within the next three months or six months or year? Pick a time frame (I really like six months — not too long, not too short) and then decide which one or two things seem reasonable to accomplish within that time frame.

Like maybe you want to move into your own place within the next six months. Or maybe you want to save X amount of dollars in the next year. Or maybe you want to make a handful of connections with some screenwriters in the next three months. (I dunno, pick something related to a career you're interested in.) Pick a time frame and pick a goal. And make it reasonable, dude. There's nothing worse than setting an overly ambitious goal only to crash and burn because it's not humanly possible.

Another way to think about this manageable goals thing is to ask yourself, *What am I willing to compromise in one area right now so that I can make progress in another area?* For example, when I graduated there were two main goals that were at the very top of my list: to build a career in a field I love, and to pay off those motherfucking student loans. And for me, getting those loans paid off felt even more urgent than finding my dream job . . . so I was willing to compromise somewhat on the dream job thing for a while in order to focus on making and saving money. I did that by holding out for a well-paying job I actually liked (even if it wasn't my dream job) so I could pay down those loans ASAP. It was only a partial compromise because there was no way I was going to take a job I hated, but it *was* a compromise. An intentional one.

It was also a compromise for my social life. The point of having a decently paying job was to make money and put it toward my loan. So I was pretty Scroogey about my spending. I was brewing my own coffee and making my lunches and mostly staying in or going out on the cheap instead of living like a baller. It meant I couldn't always do everything my friends did. But then again, some of those people are *still* paying off their loans, and I'm not (booyah!).

> There's nothing worse than setting an overly ambitious goal only to crash and burn because it's not humanly possible.

Listen, I know compromise isn't exactly sexy. Especially when we live in a society obsessed with instant gratification. But the truth is you're not going to be able to get everything you want right away, so you might as well get strategic about tackling some of your biggest priorities first. And keep in mind that *your* priorities might be different than mine, or your best friend's, or your parents'. Stay true to you, and don't let anyone throw you off course.

➡ WINNING IS FOR LOSERS ⬅

Staying true to yourself sounds nice and all, but it's actually super hard. And you know what makes it even harder? Comparing yourself to others.

If you're like most other humans on the planet, you

compare yourself to others to see how you measure up. And if you're like most other humans on the planet, doing this makes you super fucking miserable.

You know it's going to make you feel like shit, but you compare yourself to that chick you just followed on Instagram. Or to your best friend, who just bought a condo. Or to your cousin, who scored a super sweet job with a super sweet salary to match.

It's tempting to play the comparison game. But instead of helping you get your shit together, comparing yourself to everyone else just makes you want to up your anxiety meds.

If you're in the habit of getting all wound up and competitive and perfectionistic about everything, that's just going to continue later on in your life. You're basically laying the groundwork to become one of those fake-smiling, sleep-deprived soccer moms who makes picture-perfect rainbow layer cakes and cuts the kids' organic watermelon halftime snack into little heart shapes. And you don't want to be that chick. She's miserable and exhausted from doing too much and keeping up appearances.

You need to develop some *calm the hell down* habits now. That way, even if you do become a soccer mom, you'll be the kind who brings a bag of apples and says, *Have at it, kids*, while you've got it made in the shade, sipping from your travel mug coffee, which may or may not have a shot of bourbon in it.

Soccer Mom A is waaaaay too into keeping up appearances, and she's one failed Pinterest project away from cracking and having a total meltdown. Soccer Mom B, on the other hand, doesn't buy into that and is just doing her own damn thing, enjoying life. Be like Soccer Mom B.

It's way easier to ease up on comparing yourself to others if you can catch yourself in the act — if you can start to notice when and where and why you tend to play the comparison game.

Maybe you're always prying into other people's lives just to see if they have a leg up on you.

Maybe you're bugging your friends about their job hunt status, and it secretly drives you mental if they seem to be having more success than you.

Maybe you have a bad habit of creeping your old classmates on Instagram to see how you measure up.

Or maybe you post fake-ass, over-glamorized shit to make it seem like you're loving life when really you're super miserable.

Cut that shit out. Or at least curb it. Significantly. Winning is for losers. Constantly evaluating your progress and success and worthiness against other people is a really sad-ass thing to do. You are not your resume, or your job title, or your contacts, or your bank account balance, or your credit score, or some online persona. You're much more than that.

> You are not your resume, or your job title,
> or your contacts, or your bank account balance,
> or your credit score, or some online persona.

Plus, comparing yourself to others isn't actually productive. For a couple of reasons:

1. YOU'RE NOT WORKING WITH REAL INFORMATION.

You know how you take like five selfies before you post one? Your bestie comments, "Gorge!" but little does she know there were four other photos where you looked like Shrek. When you're looking in from the outside, you only see the good stuff. For example, that chick who seems like a total baller on Instagram? Her dad still pays her phone bill. And rent.

People only share the stories they *want* to share, whether it's on Instagram or over brunch. This includes a collection of carefully curated highlights about their career. Believing that someone else's highlight reel is the unfiltered truth will give you an eye twitch for a month.

2. COMPARING TAKES YOUR EYE OFF THE PRIZE.

The prize is doing what *you* want in *your* life. Even if you don't know exactly what you want, looking at what everyone else is doing doesn't help. It just makes you feel like you should do what *they're* doing. Which is kinda sad. Don't be a copycat. An imitation life isn't good enough for you. Or for anybody, for that matter. You might be a lot closer to figuring things out if you weren't so busy trying to fall in line. (Of course, you already know this, don't you?)

Tracking your progress against others almost always feels shitty. But since it's natural to be nosy about other people's lives, let's see if we can make your nosiness more productive — by swapping out *comparison* for *investigation*.

Huh?

Comparing yourself to others usually leads to a whiny pity party. *Investigating*, on the other hand, is about research. And that's something you can work with.

You could bitch and moan that your friend has a new condo and — boo freaking hoo — you don't (comparing), or you could ask her how she did it and take note (investigating). *Oh, she's been packing her lunch every day for five years and squirreling away her savings for a down payment?* Maybe you should think about a budget.

Or let's say you're super jealous because your cousin lucked out on a cool job, and why the hell hasn't that happened to you? (That's pity-party comparing.) Instead, you might ask him about his job search and find out that he applied for 10 jobs a week for two months. He got interviewed for some and passed over for several others before scoring this one. *Oh, maybe the secret to landing a great gig is busting your ass and not crossing your fingers.* Maybe you should get more serious about this.

Here's how you make the switch from plain old bitchy comparing to *investigating*. Think of a couple of people you're a little jealous of career-wise, and then do some investigating to see what their secret sauce is. Your friend with the sweet condo's secret sauce might be saving a little over a long period of time. Your cousin with the great gig's secret sauce might be applying and interviewing like a motherfucker until it pays off.

Quit whining already and pay attention. Get some useful information. Investigating and adapting a strategy can help you get closer to where you want to be. Straight-up comparing with *no* strategy and *no* action, on the other hand — not so much. That's a game you'll never win.

Plus, most of us do the comparison thing in moments when we're feeling insecure. We all just want to know, *Am I doing okay?* We look to others for assurance, but more often than not we walk away with anxiety.

So in case you need to hear it, yes, you're doing okay. You're going to be just fine. In fact, right this second you're devoting time and energy to digging deep and figuring out what's best for you. That's something a lot of people never do in their entire lifetime. You're doing more than okay. You're doing great. Just keep going.

We all just
want to know,
Am I doing okay?

⇒ DECISION AUTOPSY ⇐

As you move forward, some of the things you do are going to make you feel great. And others? Meh, not so much. It's your job to figure out why some stuff feels good and why some stuff feels bad. Because that will help you make better decisions next time.

Think of a career decision (or maybe something school-related) that didn't make you very happy. For example, I knew I was miserable in my PhD at about the two-year mark, but I didn't quit until I was four years in. I spent two whole years telling myself I had to finish this thing I hated. Bad decision. Everything told me I was headed down the wrong path, and yet I tried to force it. If I had a do-over, I'd quit sooner. I should have listened to my gut.

Maybe you went to law school even though you hated it. Maybe you did what your dad said you should do for your career even though it didn't feel right. Or maybe you stayed in a relationship that felt bad. (This stuff works for life choices, too, not just career ones.) Think back to a decision you made that didn't work out so well — one that made you say, *Oh, that didn't actually make me very happy*.

Now, *why* do you think you made that decision? And what did you learn from it? In my case (staying in the PhD when I should have quit sooner), I tried to force something that deep down I knew wasn't right for me. And I did it because I got all caught up in my fear of what other people would think, worried that I'd look like a failure if I quit. What I learned was that letting your fear of what other people might think direct the course of your life isn't worth it.

If you went to law school and hated it, it's possible that you were caught up in pursuing something lucrative and prestigious. And maybe you learned that there are things more important than that — like spending your life doing something you actually enjoy.

If you took your dad's career advice against your better judgment, it's possible that you thought it was the safest choice, or that making your dad happy would be enough to make you happy. If so, my guess is that you probably learned it's not.

We can do the same thing for a decision that you *were* happy with — like choosing an amazing school that was just the right fit, or moving to a city you love, or taking a risk on a job in a different field. Again, ask yourself why you made that decision and what you learned from it.

Maybe going to school X instead of school Y was something you never planned to do, but when you went for a campus visit, you just fell in love with it, so you changed your plans. And you learned that changing your plans can actually be a good thing.

Maybe you moved to a city you love because you wanted to be exposed to more diversity and art and culture than you had been exposed to where you grew up. You ended up loving it and learned that following adventure feels really good.

Maybe you took a risk on a job in a different field because you hated the field you studied, and even though you weren't sure if this new field was going to be a good fit, you thought it was worth a shot. You learned that taking a chance on something, even when there's some uncertainty involved, can be totally worth it.

Ask yourself why you made that decision and what you learned from it.

This process of examining your past decisions (both the ones that worked out great and the ones that didn't) is what I like to call a *decision autopsy* — looking at a decision after the fact to see where you nailed it, or where you went wrong, and what you learned from the experience. Keep doing decision autopsies as you navigate your career, and you'll become a master of making good decisions.

⚏ YOUR PERSONAL BRAND OF SELF-SABOTAGE ⚏

Once you start examining past decisions, you'll likely notice some themes around the thoughts and behaviors that have held you back.

How about perfectionism, for one? If nothing is ever good enough, you're guaranteed to always fall short. Or how about chronic avoidance using things like food or alcohol or Netflix or sleep? Keep it up, and you're guaranteed to live a life of regret. Or maybe bullying is your thing. A great way to lose friends and alienate people. Or gossiping! You could be the Regina George of the work world. Remember how happy she was?

My point? In the quest for happiness, there are 101 ways to fuck it up. Because we (you, me, and even Almighty Oprah) do all kinds of things to self-sabotage. Without even knowing it. Things like the stuff I just mentioned. Or things like procrastination, giving up too easily, being too rigid, never trying anything new, being way too self-critical, or any number of other things.

Each of us has our own personal brand of self-sabotage — a unique combination of hang-ups and behaviors that subvert and undermine the things we want.

For Vic, one of my clients, the issue was overworking. He was always on the edge of burnout. To make matters worse, he lived right across from his office building, so it was easy to work all the time. Vic was a brilliant strategy guy, but he wasn't thinking very strategically about his own productivity. He was (mistakenly) measuring his productivity in hours, not actual output. This is an outdated model of productivity, and unfortunately one that most organizations still use. The idea is the more hours you put in, the more productive you are. Makes sense, right?

Nope.

In the quest for happiness, there are 101 ways to fuck it up.

At some point you reach the point of diminishing returns — the point where more hours actually leads to shittier work that is less creative, less innovative, and filled with more errors. Because you're so fucking tired, and your brain is fried. So Vic had to create some boundaries around his work and actually work *less* in order to stop sabotaging his career.

Lana, another client, struggled with nonstop negativity in both her personal and professional life. She hated her boss and hated her job, so she spent a lot of time bitching. Bitching was a survival tactic for her. She felt angry and powerless, so she'd bitch to let off a little steam just so she could function. Unfortunately, the constant bitching and negativity was sabotaging all of her relationships. Have you ever been around someone who bitches ALL of the time?

Yeah. It's *exhausting*. You feel like a deflated balloon after spending just five minutes with them — like someone sucked the life right out of you.

Her friends, and even her partner, just couldn't handle her anymore. So Lana and I created a two-part strategy to curb the bitching pronto before her friends and family ditched her by the side of the road. First, since she found it so hard to stop complaining, she filled her evenings with activities that would distract her from bitching. (It's easy to bitch and moan about your job to your partner while you're both hunched over takeout, watching Netflix, but harder to do it when you're sweating your ass off and barely able to catch your breath in a spin class.) Part two of the strategy (and the more important bit, if you ask me) was to have Lana actually *do* something about getting out of her shitty work situation instead of just complaining about it. She had to reclaim responsibility for her life and stop playing the victim.

Oz, another client, has a personal brand of self-sabotage that is shared by many (maybe even you). He feels over-whelmed from overthinking all of the time. Because of this, he's always thinking, thinking, thinking, but rarely actually *doing* anything to improve his situation. You know that term "analysis paralysis"? That's Oz in a nutshell. He's always so caught up in planning (courses, conferences, mastermind groups, you name it) — perpetually stuck in planning and thinking — that he never has time to actually *implement* any of his plans.

The solution for Oz is to *think less* and *do more* — something that sounds simple in concept, but overthinking is a tough habit to break in practice. Overthinking is a common form of self-sabotage because it *seems* productive. But more often, it's a sneaky form of procrastination. You never have to take a risk or actually *do* anything if you're still gathering information and thinking things over, right?

Another client, Monica, had unreasonably high expectations (like *impossible* expectations) of herself and others. She was constantly angry and disappointed because everyone let her down, always falling short of what she expected of them. The problem was twofold for Monica because not only were her expectations unreasonable, but she also never clearly communicated her expectations to the people she worked with (and it's impossible for people to do what you want if you don't *tell* them what you want).

Monica's solution was a two-parter: first, to ease up on the unreasonable expectations, and second, to start clearly communicating her expectations, so that people have at least a half-decent shot at meeting them.

What's *your* own personal brand of self-sabotage — your go-to method of getting in your own way? For me, it's setting overly ambitious goals. I always try to do way too much in way too short of a time frame. Which means I'm constantly falling short of my (totally impossible) goals even when I'm kicking ass and doing really amazing shit. That doesn't feel awesome. Ambition is good, but ambition paired with a healthy dose of reality is even better. I'm getting much better at setting reasonable goals, but honestly, I'm still working on it.

If you're not already working on cooling some of your self-sabotage habits, now is the time. And if you *are* already working on them, you probably know that there are no quick fixes. No biggie. Don't beat yourself up about it. Progress is progress. Keep pursuing your career goals, but continue to work on this stuff as you go.

⇛ GOOD VIBES ONLY ⇚

So far on this Career Rookie adventure, I've been your trusty sidekick — the Bert to your Ernie, the Hermione to your Harry, the peanut butter to your jelly. But here we are in the home stretch, and it's time for you to assemble your own team of compadres to support you on your career journey. Because you don't want to do this career thing alone. And you don't have to. As you continue to move forward, you'll want a Venus to your Serena, a Timberlake to your Fallon, a Gayle to your Oprah.

The people you choose to surround yourself with will help you along. Notice I *didn't* say whoever you happen to be hanging out with, or the peeps in your immediate proximity. I said the people you *choose* to surround yourself with. Because that's a choice, you know. And most people don't even think about it.

Remember back in chapter seven when we talked about

ways to make the most of your time and energy? Well, being intentional about the people you allow into your orbit is one of the best ways you can manage your energy.

I mean, think about the magic that happens when Tina Fey and Amy Poehler join forces. And where would Han Solo have been without Chewbacca? My point is: having good-vibes people (Wookiees?) around you makes everything so much better.

You've probably noticed that you get a *good vibes* energy around some people and a *bad vibes* energy around some people. Start to notice the difference because the energy of the people around you will definitely impact your career.

If you have lunch with your friend Debbie Downer three times a week, you'll probably notice that you start to feel like a bit of a downer yourself. And another road trip with Control Freak Carol would drive you mental. But hanging with Sunny Susan makes you feel kind of warm and tingly. And hanging with Chill Charlie always makes you feel more relaxed.

Emotional contagion. It's a thing. A real, honest-to-goodness, actual scientific thing. We catch each other's emotions just like we catch each other's colds. (Which is why nobody wants to go anywhere near the stressed-out, tear-streaked, panicked chick just before final exams.) The people around you impact the way you feel. And how you feel impacts your career. Obviously.

Let's say that every time you talk to your mom she's kvetching that you don't have a job yet. Every conversation with her makes you want to get blackout drunk, just so you can stop feeling like such an eternal disappointment. She's your mom and you love her, but it might be time to switch from daily phone calls to weekly ones.

Or maybe you have a friend who bitches and moans about every little bit of (self-inflicted) drama in her life. But the minute you want to talk about your career, she totally ghosts on you. Kind of a dick move. Maybe you shouldn't include that person as a part of your inner circle.

We catch each other's emotions just like we catch each other's colds.

Is there someone in your life who is a constant energy suck, especially when it comes to your career? Someone who stresses you out and brings you down?

You don't have to cut people like this out of your life (that's especially tricky if they're family members), but you may want to reconsider how much time you spend with them. You can still love someone and spend less time with them.

What you want to do is build a squad of good-vibes people — people who support your goals and inspire you and make you feel strong. If you're lucky, you probably have some of these people around you already. Spend more time with them, and let their good vibes wash over you.

Now, there are probably some other people around you

who are totally good vibes, but who you don't know very well yet. Maybe some of these people could even help you on your career path. Who would you love to add to your good-vibes career squad, even if it's just to grab coffee and chat occasionally?

And how about adding not just people, but books, and websites, and podcasts, and other tools to help you with your career goals. Make sure you only choose ones that actually make you feel good, not ones that stress you out or bring you down. Remember, this is about creating a positive, good-vibes support squad.

Suddenly you've got more support than you thought you had! Just remember one thing: *You* are the leader of your good-vibes career squad. As amazing as these people and resources are, you're the one in the driver's seat, and the only one in charge of what you do and where you go.

IT'S GO TIME

So you have an idea about a direction you'd like to go in. It feels a bit scary, but hopefully it's the *right* kind of scary. And after all of our work together you might be thinking, *Excellent! Now all I need to do is a bunch of prep work before I make my move.*

Careful there.

Preparing is great. Just don't go overboard.

I was at the grocery store last week, and when I passed the dish soap aisle, I thought, *Maybe I better grab a bottle just in case.*

When I got home and unpacked my groceries, I went to put my dish soap in the cupboard under the sink . . . where I found *five* other bottles of dish soap. On the one hand, in the event of the zombie apocalypse, at least I'll have clean dishes. On the other hand, why on earth had I absentmindedly picked up dish soap *five* other times?

I'll tell you why: My default setting is *overprepare*. It's why I see something and think, *Maybe I should pick that up. Just in case.*

It's also why I bought *seven* big, bold necklaces to wear on television before I was even on TV once. And why I read three or four or *ten* books when I'm researching something, instead of just one. I always think, *I'm not quite ready yet. Maybe I should prepare a little more. Just in case.*

I bet you do this, too. You think maybe you should do some more research or read another book or listen to another podcast or take another class (or a whole other degree) before you make your move. Just in case.

The truth is some preparation is totally unnecessary. Once you pass a certain threshold, it's redundant. Like when you already have five bottles of dish soap at home but you think, *Maybe I oughta get one just in case.* Or when you're subscribing to your 12th podcast about art and design, but you won't let yourself sign up for that art class that you've been stalking for months. Or when you have a whole library full of books about entrepreneurship, but you haven't pulled the trigger on your own business yet. Or when you've looked through about 1,000 job postings, but still haven't applied for a single one.

Sometimes preparation is just cleverly disguised procrastination.

You've probably prepared enough. It's go time. Time to start. The best advice I can give you is to start *anywhere*, be it a big leap or a baby step. Don't just think, DO. And start before you think you're ready. I suggest now.

Yes, you're scared, and some of the details are still fuzzy, but time is wasting. And you've come too far to chicken out now.

Sending you oodles of good vibes for your career journey.

XO SARAH

PS — For a loving push and a little extra help, grab the free resources for Career Rookies at careergasm.com.

THANK YOU

A lot of love went into this book. Jen Knoch and Stacy Testa, thank your for being my ride-or-die babes in the publishing process — for your thoughtful guidance, your faith in me, and for rolling with me when I was a hot mess. Thanks also to Crissy Calhoun and Avril McMeekin for your brilliant brains and keen eyes. This book is better because of you. Susannah Ames, thank you for your kindness and enthusiasm and hustle. And to the whole posse of quirky oddballs at ECW Press, thank you. I adore you.

To the lovely humans at WeWork, Tangerine, Artscape, and Evergreen Brickworks, thank you for providing space and support for me to do my work. Sandy Chronopoulos, Tracy Moore, Carolyn Graham and the whole team at *Cityline*, thank you for making careers a part of the conversation and for trusting me to not swear on national television. (So far, so good!)

Thank you to the people who helped me find my way when I was a career rookie, myself. Charmaine Hack and Susan Vercruysse, I thank my lucky stars that I encountered strong women like you so early in my career. I was paying attention. Thank you. Laurie Barclay and Simon Taggar, thank you for being a safe place when I felt lost, and for listening instead of telling me what to do. Glenda Burrell, Marybeth Jantzi, and Pat Gibbings, thank you for showing me how to write and speak and stand up and be seen before I even knew how important that was.

Emma Buckley, thank you for being one of the engines behind Careergasm. I trust you completely and that's saying something. Phil Rickaby, thank you for always answering my panicked texts and for making things okay when I'm on the edge of a code red meltdown.

To my friends — Sarah Joore, Ashley De Filippis, Shawn Phelps, Phil Rickaby (yes, again), Jayne Fleming, Samantha Read, Marion Langford, Kristian Nasager, Brigid Dineen, Laura Jensen, Dean Williams, and Gwen Elliot — thank you for cheering me on in good times and for scraping me off the floor when shit gets ugly. Riley Skelton, thank you for being the bright, shiny human that you are.

Thank you Mom and Dad. You always let me find my own way and it turns out that's a rare and precious gift. And thanks to the rest of my family — Brian, Brad, Dan, Scottie, Ashley, Nicole, Lisa, Liv, Ethan, and Brooklynn. I feel lucky that I get to walk through life with you.

To my clients, thank you for trusting me with your tender hearts. Your bravery and your commitment to make the most of this life inspires me on a daily basis. And thank you, dear reader. We may not have met, but I was holding you in my heart as I wrote this. I hope it helped you.

SARAH VERMUNT is the founder of Careergasm and the author of *Careergasm: Find Your Way to Feel-Good Work*. Sarah is a regular career columnist on TV's *CityLine*, and her work has been featured in *Forbes, Fortune, Inc., Entrepreneur*, and *Fast Company*. She lives in Toronto, Ontario, and online at Careergasm.com.

 @careergasm

 /careergasm

 @careergasm